Williams-Sonoma's

Gifts from the Kitchen

GENERAL EDITOR
CHUCK WILLIAMS

RECIPES
KRISTINE KIDD

PHOTOGRAPHY
ALLAN ROSENBERG

TIME
LIFE
BOOKS

Time-Life Books is a division of
TIME LIFE INCORPORATED

President and CEO: John M. Fahey, Jr.
President, Time-Life Books: John D. Hall

TIME-LIFE CUSTOM PUBLISHING

Vice President and Publisher: Terry Newell
Sales Director: Frances C. Mangan
Editorial Director: Robert A. Doyle

WILLIAMS-SONOMA
Founder/Vice-Chairman: Chuck Williams

WELDON OWEN INC.
President: John Owen
Publisher: Wendely Harvey
Managing Editor: Laurie Wertz
Consulting Editor: Norman Kolpas
Copy Editor: Sharon Silva
Editorial Assistant: Janique Poncelet
Design: John Bull, The Book Design Company
Production: James Obata, Stephanie Sherman,
    Mick Bagnato
Food Photographer: Allan Rosenberg
Additional Food Photography: Allen V. Lott
Primary Food & Prop Stylist: Sandra Griswold
Food Stylist: Heidi Gintner
Assistant Food Stylist: Mara Barot
Prop Assistant: Elizabeth Ruegg
Glossary Illustrations: Alice Harth

The Williams-Sonoma Kitchen Library
conceived and produced by Weldon Owen Inc.
814 Montgomery St., San Francisco, CA 94133

In collaboration with Williams-Sonoma
100 North Point, San Francisco, CA 94133

Production by Mandarin Offset, Hong Kong
Printed in China

A Note on Weights and Measures:
All recipes include customary U.S. and metric
measurements. Metric conversions are based on
a standard developed for these books and have
been rounded off. Actual weights may vary.

A Weldon Owen Production

Copyright © 1994 Weldon Owen Inc.
Reprinted in 1994

Library of Congress
Cataloging-in-Publication Data:

Kidd, Kristine.
    Gifts from the kitchen / general editor, Chuck Williams ;
recipes, Kristine Kidd ; photography, Allan Rosenberg.
        p.   cm. — (Williams-Sonoma kitchen library)
    Includes index.
    ISBN 0-7835-0295-8
    1. Cookery.   2. Gifts.   I. Williams, Chuck.   II. Title.
III. Series.
TX652.K4346   1994
641.5—dc20   93-48176
                                    CIP

Contents

Introduction 4   Equipment 6   Finishing Touches 8
Canning Basics 10   Gift Wrapping 12

CANDIES & CONFECTIONS 15

BAKED GIFTS 39

SAVORIES 67

CANNED GIFTS 85

Glossary 104   Acknowledgments 108   Index 108

INTRODUCTION

Not so many years ago, it was customary to bring a gift of food when paying a special visit to a neighbor or a member of the family. On holidays, too, gifts of homemade food were not merely economic necessities, but true expressions of a heartfelt desire to share good things with others.

The art and custom of giving gifts of food has, I fear, been neglected of late. That is why I am especially pleased to introduce this volume of recipes that are expressly created to be given to others.

Flip through the following pages and you'll encounter dozens of great ideas for delicious presents you can make in your own kitchen: sweet and savory baked goods, candies, spreads, sauces and condiments. The book's introductory lessons will guide you through the basics of canning recipes to prolong their shelf life; icing and decorating cakes and cookies; and gift-wrapping ideas to give food a more festive appearance and to keep it in peak condition. An illustrated glossary at the end of the book answers your questions on unusual ingredients and techniques called for in the recipes.

Let me call your attention to one distinctive feature of the book that I find particularly gratifying. The recipe photographs purposely show the foods both prepared as gifts and actually in use. These images are intended to inspire you not just to make the recipes for giving away, but also to prepare them as special pleasures for yourself. Many of the recipes are excellent additions to any home pantry.

For anyone who loves to give—or receive—food, no matter the time of year, the recipes and instructions in this book will provide inspiration for gifts that truly come from the heart. I hope you prepare—and enjoy—some of them soon.

Chuck Williams

EQUIPMENT

A diverse array of tools assist in the preparation of sweet and savory edible gifts

Gifts of food are made by a variety of methods, from simmering to baking, melting to molding. So, in order to prepare all the recipes in this book, you would need a kitchen equipped with a wide array of tools.

But it is not necessary to go out and buy every single piece of equipment you see on these pages. Instead, select the recipe or recipes you want to prepare as gifts. Then, just as you take stock of your refrigerator and pantry to draw up a shopping list of ingredients, survey your kitchen's shelves and drawers and jot down any cookware or utensils you might be missing to complete the specific recipe. In this way, little by little, you'll build up a formidable arsenal of gift-making tools.

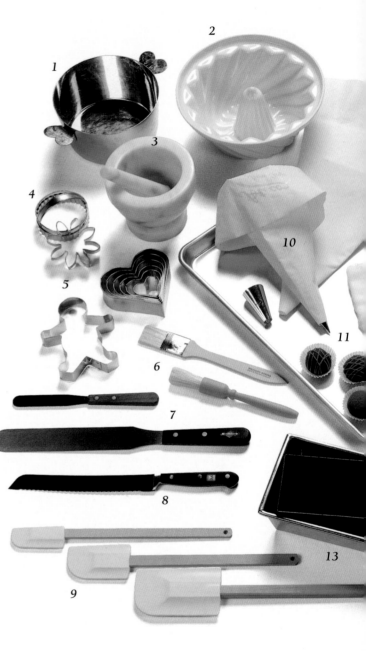

1. Charlotte Mold
Traditional French bucket-shaped tinned-steel container, ideal for molding iced desserts and custards as well as for baking cylindrical loaves such as the Italian holiday bread *panettone*.

2. Bundt Pan
Fluted tube pan for baking festive ring-shaped cakes.

3. Mortar and Pestle
For crushing and grinding dried herbs and spices by hand. Marble mortar provides stable weight; its unpolished bowl gives a good grinding sur-face. Brass, glass and ceramic models are also available.

4. Biscuit Cutter
Wide circular cutter with fluted edge for decoratively cutting out dough for scones or biscuits.

5. Cookie Cutters
Sturdy tinned or stainless-steel cutters provide a wide variety of attractive shapes.

6. Pastry Brushes
For brushing glazes onto baked goods, and for washing down the sides of saucepans to keep crystals from forming in sugar syrups.

7. Spatulas
Small, narrow-bladed spatula neatly spreads icings or other cookie or cake toppings, and accurately levels the surface of dry ingredients with the rims of measuring cups. Larger spatula efficiently removes cookies from baking sheets and pans.

8. Serrated Knife
Long, sturdy, serrated blade for slicing biscotti before their final baking.

9. Rubber Spatulas

For folding batters, scraping them out of mixing bowls and smoothing their surfaces in baking pans; also for smoothing the surfaces of fudges and other pan-molded candies. Choose sturdy, pliable rubber or silicone heads.

10. Pastry Bags and Tips

Plastic-lined cloth or all-plastic bags and stainless-steel tips enable easy, accurate piping of soft cookie doughs or decorative icings. Choose larger bags, which are easier to fill and handle.

11. Baking Sheet

For baking cookies and for holding candies as they are shaped and set.

12. Cheesecloth

For forming sachets to contain mulling spices.

13. Loaf Pans

For baking large and individual-sized loaf-shaped cakes and quick breads. Choose good-quality heavy aluminum or tinplate steel, which conducts heat well for fast, even baking.

14. Canning Pot

Large, heavy enameled or stainless-steel pot with tight-fitting lid and fitted wire rack that holds filled canning jars securely in place while they are boiled (pages 10–11).

15. Canning Jars

Sturdy, wide-mouthed glass jars made specifically for canning purposes, with lids and separate screw-on bands that form an airtight vacuum during the canning process. Be sure to use only lids and bands manufactured specifically for the jars you are using. Do not reuse lids, which cannot form a seal once they have been opened.

16. Funnels

Sturdy, heatproof metal funnels assist in neatly pouring hot mixtures into canning jars and bottles.

17. Wire Strainer

Fine-mesh sieve for straining solids from jams, curds and other canned gifts.

18. Jar Tongs

Large, sturdy tongs with heatproof handles safely and securely remove hot jars from canning pots.

19. Candy Thermometer

Clips to the side of a saucepan for gauging the temperature of a candy mixture or flavored vinegar. Because readings will vary with altitude, calibrate your thermometer by using it to measure the temperature of boiling water. The difference between your reading and 212°F (100°C) should be applied to the temperatures given in the recipes.

20. Parchment Paper

Stick-resistant, ovenproof paper for lining baking sheets.

21. Kitchen String

For tying sachets for mulling spices.

22. Candy Cups

Individual fluted cups of plain or decorated paper or foil, for holding individual candies while they set and for presentation.

FINISHING TOUCHES

Baked goods intended for gifts become even more festive when finished with a glaze, coating or icing—a simple task given the basic recipes shown here and the ease with which they can be spread or piped to decorative effect (see photos, opposite).

LEMON GLAZE

An easy-to-make glaze that gives a pretty, professional look to cakes or quick breads.

1½ cups (6 oz/185 g) confectioners' (icing) sugar, sifted after measuring
2 tablespoons unsalted butter, melted
1 tablespoon fresh lemon juice
½ teaspoon vanilla extract (essence)
1 tablespoon boiling water

*I*n a bowl, combine the sugar, melted butter, lemon juice and vanilla. Gradually add the boiling water, stirring with a spoon until smooth and spreadable.

Use a rubber spatula to spread the glaze over cooled cakes or breads.

Makes about ¾ cup (6 fl oz/180 ml)

CHOCOLATE COATING

You can give a lovely finish to a number of the cookies in this collection by spreading or drizzling them with this delicious coating. If possible, use a European chocolate, which generally results in better flavor and texture.

8 oz (250 g) semisweet or bittersweet chocolate, chopped

*P*lace the chocolate in the top pan of a double boiler or in a heatproof bowl. Set over (but not touching) simmering water and heat, stirring frequently, until melted and smooth. Remove from the heat.

To coat cookie tops with the chocolate, use the back of a spoon to spread it evenly on the tops.

To drizzle the chocolate decoratively over the cookies, dip the tines of a fork into the chocolate and wave them back and forth over the cookies.

Refrigerate all chocolate-coated cookies until the chocolate sets. Then transfer to a covered container and store in the refrigerator.

Makes about ¾ cup (6 fl oz/180 ml)

Currant, Lemon and Ginger Cakes

Vanilla and Walnut Shortbread Hearts

CONFECTIONERS' SUGAR ICING

Naturally off-white, this basic icing can be used as is or tinted with food coloring to give a wide variety of finished looks to your holiday cookies. Spread it onto cookies and then sprinkle with colored sugar crystals, or pipe it from a pastry bag in decorative patterns.

3 cups (12 oz/375 g) confectioners' (icing) sugar
2 tablespoons milk, or as needed
1½ tablespoons fresh lemon juice
food coloring, optional
colored sugar crystals, optional

Place the confectioners' sugar in a bowl. Add the 2 tablespoons milk and the lemon juice and stir until smooth. If the mixture is too thick to pipe or spread, thin with a small amount of additional milk.

To color the icing, mix in the food coloring, adding it by drops until the desired shade is achieved. Alternatively, divide the icing among several bowls and tint each portion a different color.

To spread the icing over cookies, use a small icing spatula or a small knife.

To pipe the icing atop cookies, spoon the icing into a pastry bag fitted with a small plain tip. Pipe decoratively over the cookies.

To drizzle the icing over cookies, dip a fork into the icing and wave it back and forth over the cookies.

To decorate the icing-topped cookies with colored sugar, sprinkle on the sugar as soon as the cookies are iced.

Place the cookies on a flat surface until the icing sets, about 2 hours. Store iced cookies in an airtight container at room temperature.

Makes about 1 cup (8 fl oz/250 ml)

DECORATING WITH ICING

Spreading icing.
Once the cookies have cooled completely, use a small icing spatula—shown here—or a small knife to scoop up some of the icing and spread it neatly and evenly over each cookie.

Piping icing.
For a more decorative effect, spoon the icing into a pastry bag fitted with a small plain tip. Fold down the top of the bag and, applying even pressure, squeeze out the icing to form an attractive pattern.

Holiday Orange-Spice Cutouts

Canning Basics

Canning—preserving jars of food by boiling them in water—daunts some home cooks with its strict rules. But those rules are necessary to safeguard against spoilage. Extended boiling ensures that all enzymes and microorganisms present in the food are destroyed by heat—and, with special canning lids and screw bands, forms a partial vacuum seal that prevents microorganisms from entering the jars and contaminating the food.

The length of time filled and sealed jars are boiled depends upon the ingredients being canned. In this book, foods processed in a hot-water bath boil for 15 minutes. Other recipes such as those for flavored oils and honeys simply call for sterilizing the containers (see below).

Successfully canned foods in which a tight seal has formed (step 4, opposite) will keep at cool room temperature for up to a year. Once a jar's contents have been eaten, the jar and its screw band can be reused; but the lid, which will no longer form a secure seal, should be discarded.

When preparing foods for gift giving, it is always important to include a card or label with instructions for storage, such as, "Store in a cupboard for up to 1 year." If a gift requires refrigeration, it is essential to include this information as well ("Keep refrigerated for up to 2 weeks").

Sterilizing Jars and Lids

If preserves or other foods will not be processed in a hot-water bath and they will be kept at room temperature, the jars must be sterilized before they are filled. Follow this simple method.

Thoroughly wash jars and their lids (or other containers such as bottles) in hot soapy water; rinse well. Place the jars upright on a metal rack in a large pot. Fill the pot and jars with hot (not boiling) water to cover the jars by 1 inch (2.5 cm). At altitudes of less than 1,000 feet (300 meters) above sea level, boil for 10 minutes. At higher elevations, boil an additional minute for each additional 1,000 feet.

Place the lids in a small saucepan. Cover with water and bring to a simmer. Remove the pan from the heat. Allow the jars and lids to remain in hot water until ready to use.

1. Sterilizing jars.
Place washed and rinsed jars upright on a metal rack in a large pot. Add hot water to cover by 1 inch (2.5 cm). Bring to a boil and boil for 10 minutes at altitudes less than 1,000 feet (300 meters), adding 1 minute for each additional 1,000 feet. Leave in hot water until ready to use.

2. Sterilizing lids.
Put washed and rinsed lids and screw bands in a small saucepan. Add water to cover and bring to a simmer, then remove from the heat. Leave lids and screw bands in hot water until ready to use.

Hot-Water Bath for Canning

All of the preserves in this book can be made without a water bath and stored safely in the refrigerator for up to 3 weeks. If you want to make preserves that can be kept longer at room temperature, however, follow this simple procedure. No matter which method you use, attach a gift card with the appropriate storage time.

Place a metal rack in a large pot. Set the filled, capped jars on the rack. Pour in enough boiling water to cover the jars by at least 1 inch (2.5 cm). Cover the pot and boil for 15 minutes.

Using jar tongs, transfer the jars from the water bath to a metal cooling rack. Let cool to room temperature. Using your fingertips, press on the center of each lid. If the lid stays down, the jar is sealed. Label and date and store in a cool, dry place for up to 1 year. Refrigerate after opening. If the lid pops up, store the jar in the refrigerator and use within the time specified if no water bath has been used.

Plum-Vanilla Preserves

1. Filling a canning jar.
Remove one jar from hot water, drain and fill with the food to be canned. A canning funnel is helpful for filling jars. Remove one lid from hot water, align it on top and seal tightly with a screw band.

2. Processing filled jars.
Place filled and closed jars on a metal rack in a large pot. The jars must not be touching. Pour in enough boiling water to cover by at least 1 inch (2.5 cm). Cover the pot, bring to a boil and boil for 15 minutes.

3. Cooling the jars.
With jar tongs, remove the jars from the pot and put on a metal cooling rack. Let stand at room temperature to cool, during which time the lids may give off a pinging sound—indicating that they are forming vacuum seals.

4. Testing the seal.
Press down on the center of the lid and then lift your finger. If the lid stays down, the jar is sealed and can be stored in a cool, dry place for up to 1 year. If it pops back up, no seal has formed; refrigerate no longer than the time specified in the recipe.

GIFT WRAPPING

An assortment of imaginative options move gift wrapping beyond the realm of mere ribbon and wrapping paper

You'll locate the decorative accessories shown here in shops carrying party supplies and kitchen equipment. Let the few simple suggestions you find on these pages—and in the photographs throughout the book—inspire you to create your own gift-wrapping ideas.

1. Gift Boxes
A selection of small and large boxes with lids, made of such sturdy yet reasonably priced materials as cardboard and straw, for packing cookies and candies.

2. Baskets
An attractive assortment of large and small baskets made from straw, wood or other materials, for packaging sturdy items such as individually wrapped candies, cookies and breads.

3. Tin Pails
Sturdy metal pails hold cookies, candies, breadsticks or other small items.

4. Gift Bags
Attractively printed sturdy paper bags in a wide range of festive patterns, complete with built-in ties, for filling with biscotti or other fairly sturdy items.

5. Ribbons, Strings and Cords
An assortment of supplies for securing or decoratively tying gift containers.

6. Gift Tags and Labels
Tie-on and self-adhesive tags and labels, for showing recipients' names and for providing instructions on keeping times and how to serve or cook edible gifts.

7. Stamps and Stamp Pad
Inexpensive way to add festive, personalized decorations to gift cards and wrapping paper. For an especially dazzling effect, seek out stamp pads saturated with metallic gold or silver ink.

8. Seals and Sealing Wax
A traditional way to seal gifts with a personal touch: Light the wick of the candlelike stick of wax and let the wax drip onto the knot or package seam to be sealed. Then press the metal seal into the cooling wax to leave an impression.

9. Paper Doilies
Inexpensive, lacey paper doilies attractively line gift containers and separate layers of cookies or candies.

10. Airtight Tins
Metal containers with tight-fitting lids, for packing cookies, nuts, popcorn or other gifts.

11. Airtight Bottles
Assortment of stoppered glass bottles, including some covered in straw, for holding flavored vinegars and oils.

12. Airtight Canister
For securely packing spiced nuts, olives, potpourri or other bulky items.

13. Glass Jars
Jars in assorted sizes to hold sauces and condiments. For preserves, use specially manufactured jars that allow you to test the seal (see page 11).

14. Tissue Papers
For lining gift boxes and baskets and for wrapping bottles, jars and canisters.

15. Cellophane
For wrapping baskets and plates of food, as well as individual breads, cakes and candies.

Vanilla Bean Caramels

vegetable oil

½ cup (3½ oz/105 g) firmly packed
  golden brown sugar

½ cup (4 oz/125 g) granulated sugar

½ cup (4 fl oz/125 ml) light corn syrup

¼ cup (2 fl oz/60 ml) plus 2 tablespoons whole milk

¼ cup (2 fl oz/60 ml) plus 2 tablespoons condensed milk

¼ cup (2 fl oz/60 ml) heavy (double)
  cream

¼ cup (2 oz/60 g) unsalted butter

1 vanilla bean, split lengthwise

pinch of salt

Walnut lovers might want to stir 1½ cups (6 oz/185 g) chopped wal-nuts into the caramel after removing the vanilla bean (make certain to stir gently). You will need 3 dozen pieces of cellophane, waxed paper or colored waxed paper (sold at kitchenware shops)—each measuring 4½ by 6 inches (12 by 15 cm)—for wrapping the caramels.

Line an 8-inch (20-cm) square baking pan with foil, covering the bottom and sides. Brush generously with vegetable oil.

In a heavy 3-qt (3-l) saucepan over medium heat, combine the brown sugar, granulated sugar, corn syrup, whole milk, condensed milk, cream, butter, vanilla bean and salt. Stir constantly until the sugar dissolves and the mixture comes to a boil. Using a pastry brush dipped in water, brush down the sides of the pan to prevent sugar crystals from forming. Raise the heat to medium-high and clip a candy thermometer onto the side of the pan. Cook, stirring slowly but constantly, until the thermometer registers 240°F (116°C), about 10 minutes.

Remove the pan from the heat. Remove the vanilla bean and discard. Immediately pour the caramel into the prepared pan all at once; do not scrape the residue from the pan bottom. Let the caramel cool completely, about 2 hours.

Coat a cutting board with vegetable oil. Turn out the cooled caramel onto the board and peel off the foil. Oil a large knife and cut the caramel into strips about 1½ inches (4 cm) wide. Cut the strips crosswise into pieces 1 inch (2.5 cm) long, reoiling the knife occasionally to prevent sticking. Wrap each candy in a piece of clear cellophane, waxed paper or colored waxed paper (see note), twisting the ends. Store in an airtight container at room temperature for up to 2 weeks.

Makes about 3 dozen

Milk Chocolate and Toasted-Almond Fudge

1 oz (30 g) unsweetened chocolate,
chopped

6 oz (185 g) milk chocolate, preferably
European, chopped

1 teaspoon vanilla extract (essence)

1½ cups (12 oz/375 g) granulated sugar

⅔ cup (5 fl oz/160 ml) sweetened
condensed milk

⅔ cup (5 fl oz/160 ml) water

½ cup (4 fl oz/125 ml) heavy (double)
cream

¼ cup (2 oz/60 g) unsalted butter,
cut into pieces

¾ cup (4 oz/125 g) whole almonds,
toasted and very coarsely chopped,
plus 28 whole almonds, toasted

Any other nut would also be great in these candies. Purchase a European milk chocolate for the best results.

Line a 5-by-9-by-3-inch (13-by-23-by-7.5-cm) loaf pan with aluminum foil, allowing the foil to overhang the sides slightly.

In a metal bowl, combine the unsweetened and milk chocolates and the vanilla; set aside. In a heavy 3-qt (3-l) saucepan over medium-low heat, combine the sugar, condensed milk, water, cream and butter. Stir until the sugar dissolves. Using a pastry brush dipped in water, brush down the sides of the pan to prevent sugar crystals from forming. Raise the heat to high and bring the mixture to a rolling boil. Reduce the heat to medium-high and clip a candy thermometer onto the side of the pan. Using a wooden spoon, stir constantly but slowly until the thermometer registers 230°F (110°C), about 16 minutes.

Pour the boiling mixture over the chocolate; do not scrape the syrupy residue from the pan bottom. Stir vigorously with a wooden spoon until the chocolate melts and the fudge thickens slightly, about 1 minute. Mix in the ¾ cup (4 oz/125 g) chopped almonds. Pour immediately into the prepared pan and smooth with a rubber spatula. Then immediately press the whole almonds into the surface, spacing evenly. Refrigerate uncovered until firm enough to cut, about 1 hour.

Using the foil overhang as an aid, lift the fudge from the pan. Peel the foil from the sides. Trim the edges of the fudge evenly and cut into 28 pieces. Store in an airtight container in the refrigerator for up to 2 weeks. Serve at room temperature.

Makes 28 pieces

Walnut-Date Clusters

1½ cups (6 oz/185 g) coarsely chopped
  pitted dates
1½ cups (6 oz/185 g) coarsely chopped
  walnuts
12 oz (375 g) milk chocolate, preferably
  European, finely chopped

*Just a few ingredients are turned into a delightful confection.
Place these sweet treats in candy cups and pack into gift tins.*

*L*ine a baking sheet with parchment paper or waxed
paper.

  In a bowl, mix together the dates and walnuts; set aside.
Place the chocolate in the top pan of a double boiler or in a
heatproof bowl. Set over (but not touching) hot (not
simmering) water. Heat, stirring constantly, until melted
and smooth.

  Pour out the hot water from the bottom pan and replace
it with lukewarm water. Replace the top pan or heatproof
bowl. Let the chocolate stand, stirring frequently, until it
cools slightly and begins to thicken, about 10 minutes.

  Stir the date-walnut mixture into the chocolate, mixing
thoroughly. Using a small spoon, scoop out slightly
rounded teaspoonfuls of the mixture and drop onto the
prepared sheet, spacing evenly. Refrigerate uncovered until
set, about 2 hours.

  Store in an airtight container in the refrigerator for up to
1 month or in the freezer for up to 2 months.

Makes about 4 dozen

Caramel-Nut Popcorn

3 qt (3 l) freshly popped corn
(about ½ cup/3 oz/90 g unpopped)

1 cup (5 oz/155 g) unsalted roasted
cashews

1 cup (5 oz/155 g) salted roasted
macadamia nuts

1 cup (5½ oz/170 g) whole almonds or
(4 oz/125 g) pecan halves

1 cup (7 oz/220 g) firmly packed dark
brown sugar

½ cup (4 fl oz/125 ml) light corn syrup

½ cup (4 oz/125 g) butter

1 tablespoon finely grated orange zest

½ teaspoon salt

1 teaspoon vanilla extract (essence)

½ teaspoon baking soda (bicarbonate
of soda)

This is likely the most luxurious popcorn you could ever want. To take it a step further, spread the clumps (after baking and cooling) on a baking sheet and drizzle with chocolate coating (recipe on page 8); be sure to store the chocolate-coated popcorn in the refrigerator.

Preheat an oven to 250°F (120°C). Butter a large roasting pan. Combine the popped corn and nuts in the prepared pan, mixing well. Place in the heating oven while preparing the glaze.

In a large heavy saucepan over medium heat, combine the brown sugar, corn syrup, butter, orange zest and salt. Bring to a boil, stirring constantly until the sugar dissolves. Boil for 4 minutes without stirring. Remove from the heat and mix in the vanilla and baking soda. Gradually pour the glaze over the popped corn mixture, stirring to coat well.

Bake until dry, stirring occasionally, about 1 hour. Remove from the oven. Using a metal spatula, free the popcorn from the bottom of the pan. Let cool completely in the pan.

Break into clumps. Store in an airtight container at room temperature for up to 1 week.

Makes about 4 qt (4 l)

Chocolate-Almond Caramels

about 1¼ cups (10 fl oz/310 ml) heavy
  (double) cream
3 tablespoons freshly ground (medium-
  grind) coffee (not instant)
3 oz (90 g) unsweetened chocolate,
  chopped
1½ cups (12 oz/375 g) granulated sugar
¾ cup (6 fl oz/180 ml) light corn syrup
¼ cup (2 oz/60 g) unsalted butter
2 teaspoons vanilla extract (essence)
¼ teaspoon salt
1¾ cups (9½ oz/305 g) whole almonds,
  toasted and coarsely chopped
vegetable oil

These rich candies have grown-up flavor. Try presenting them on plates wrapped in festive cellophane.

Line a 9-inch (23-cm) square baking pan with aluminum foil, covering the bottom and sides. Generously butter the foil.

In a heavy 3-qt (3-l) saucepan over medium-high heat, combine 1 cup (8 fl oz/250 ml) of the cream and the coffee. Bring to a boil, then remove from the heat. Cover and let steep for 30 minutes.

Return the pan to medium-high heat and bring the cream-coffee mixture to a boil again. Strain through a very fine-mesh sieve into a measuring cup. Add enough cream to measure 1 cup (8 fl oz/250 ml). Return to the saucepan and add the chocolate, sugar, corn syrup and butter. Stir over medium heat until the chocolate and butter melt and the sugar dissolves. Clip a candy thermometer onto the side of the pan and boil, gently stirring occasionally, until the thermometer registers 242°F (117°C), about 10 minutes.

Remove the pan from the heat and stir in the vanilla, salt and almonds. Pour the mixture into the prepared pan. Let cool until firm enough to cut, about 2 hours.

Coat a cutting board with vegetable oil. Turn out the cooled caramel onto the board and peel off the foil. Oil a large knife and cut the caramel into pieces about 1 inch (2.5 cm) square, reoiling the knife occasionally to prevent sticking. Wrap each square in a piece of clear cellophane or waxed paper, twisting the ends. Store in an airtight container at room temperature for up to 1 month.

Makes about 6 dozen

Pine Nut Brittle

1 cup (5 oz/155 g) pine nuts
1 tablespoon finely grated orange zest
1½ teaspoons unsalted butter
¼ teaspoon salt
1 cup (8 oz/250 g) granulated sugar
⅓ cup (3 fl oz/80 ml) water

The secret to making good brittle is low humidity, since the candy becomes sticky in humid weather. So wait for a dry day, then whip up a batch of this old favorite, which has been given a twist with the addition of pine nuts and orange zest. Pack the finished product in airtight glass jars tied with ribbon.

*B*utter a baking sheet. In a bowl, combine the pine nuts, orange zest, butter and salt. Set aside.

In a heavy 2-qt (2-l) saucepan over low heat, combine the sugar and the water. Stir constantly until the sugar dissolves. Using a pastry brush dipped in water, brush down the sides of the pan to prevent sugar crystals from forming. Raise the heat to high and bring the mixture to a rolling boil. Continue to boil without stirring, swirling the pan occasionally, until the mixture turns a deep golden color, about 10 minutes.

Add the nut mixture and stir until coated with the syrup. Immediately pour onto the buttered baking sheet. Spread out slightly with a wooden spoon, forming a thin sheet of brittle. Let cool completely, about 30 minutes.

Break into pieces. Store in an airtight container at room temperature for up to 1 week.

Makes about 10 oz (315 g)

Double-Chocolate and Orange Truffles

12 oz (375 g) European milk chocolate, chopped

½ cup (4 fl oz/125 ml) frozen orange juice concentrate, thawed

2 tablespoons unsalted butter, at room temperature

unsweetened cocoa powder

12 oz (375 g) bittersweet or semisweet chocolate, finely chopped

To give these an extra-special touch, dust with cocoa powder or drizzle with melted milk chocolate.

In a heavy saucepan over medium-low heat, combine the milk chocolate and orange juice concentrate. Stir constantly until smooth. Add the butter and stir until incorporated. Pour into a bowl; this mixture is the truffle filling. Cover and freeze until firm enough to mound in a spoon, about 40 minutes.

Line a baking sheet with foil. Using a tablespoon, scoop out rounded spoonfuls of the filling and drop onto the sheet, spacing evenly. Cover and freeze until almost firm but still pliable, about 30 minutes. Roll each chocolate mound between your palms into a smooth ball, then roll in cocoa. Return to the sheet. Freeze while preparing the coating.

Line another baking sheet with foil. Place the bittersweet or semisweet chocolate in the top pan of a double boiler or in a heatproof bowl. Set over (but not touching) barely simmering water. Heat, stirring frequently, until melted and smooth. Remove from the heat.

Drop 1 truffle ball into the chocolate, tilting the pan if necessary to coat the ball completely. Slip a fork under the truffle, lift it from the chocolate and tap the fork gently against the side of the pan to allow any excess chocolate to drip off. Using a knife, gently slide the truffle off the fork and onto the prepared baking sheet. Repeat with the remaining truffles.

Refrigerate uncovered until firm, about 1 hour. Store in an airtight container in the refrigerator for up to 3 weeks.

Makes about 1½ dozen

Espresso, White Chocolate and Macadamia Nut Bark

10 oz (315 g) European white
   chocolate, finely chopped
8 oz (250 g) bittersweet or semisweet
   chocolate, finely chopped
1¾ cups (9 oz/280 g) unsalted
   macadamia nuts, toasted and halved
2 teaspoons freshly ground (fine-grind)
   coffee (not instant)

If you prefer, chopped toasted almonds can be substituted for the macadamia nuts. Either way, the result is an elegant, beautifully marbled after-dinner candy. Purchase a European-made white chocolate such as Lindt or Callebaut for the best texture.

*B*utter a 15-by-10-inch (37.5-by-25-cm) jelly-roll pan. Line with waxed paper.

Place the white chocolate in the top pan of a double boiler or in a heatproof bowl. Set over (but not touching) barely simmering water. Place the bittersweet or semisweet chocolate in the top pan of another double boiler or in a heatproof bowl set over (but not touching) barely simmering water. Stir both frequently until melted and smooth.

Stir ¾ cup (4 oz/120 g) of the nuts into the white chocolate. Pour the white chocolate onto the prepared jelly-roll pan to form 3 stripes the full length of the pan, one down each side and one down the center. Mix ½ cup (2½ oz/80 g) of the nuts and the coffee into the bittersweet or semisweet chocolate. Pour this chocolate onto the prepared pan, forming 2 stripes the length of the pan, between the white chocolate stripes. Draw the tip of a small knife back and forth across both chocolates to form a marble pattern. Tilt the pan to swirl the chocolates together. Sprinkle with the remaining ½ cup (2½ oz/80 g) nuts. Refrigerate uncovered until firm, at least 1 hour.

Gently peel the candy from the waxed paper. Holding the candy with the waxed paper (to prevent fingerprints on the chocolate), break into large irregular pieces. Store in an airtight container in the refrigerator for up to 2 weeks.

Makes about 1⅓ lb (660 g)

Walnut-Raisin Fudge

¾ cup (3 oz/90 g) coarsely chopped
   toasted walnuts
¾ cup (4½ oz/140 g) raisins
3 tablespoons finely grated orange zest
6 oz (185 g) bittersweet or semisweet
   chocolate, chopped
1½ oz (45 g) unsweetened chocolate,
   chopped
¼ cup (¾ oz/20 g) marshmallow creme
1 teaspoon vanilla extract (essence)
1½ cups (12 oz/375 g) granulated sugar
¾ cup (6 fl oz/180 ml) sweetened
   condensed milk
⅓ cup (3 fl oz/80 ml) water
⅓ cup (3 fl oz/80 ml) heavy (double)
   cream
¼ cup (2 oz/60 g) unsalted butter, cut
   into ½-inch (12-mm) pieces
32 walnut halves

This recipe for no-fail fudge calls for purchased marshmallow creme, making preparation even easier.

Line a 5-by-9-by-3-inch (13-by-23-by-7.5-cm) loaf pan with aluminum foil, allowing the foil to overhang the sides slightly.

In a small bowl, mix together the ¾ cup (3 oz/90 g) chopped walnuts, the raisins and orange zest; set aside. In a metal bowl, stir together the bittersweet or semisweet and the unsweetened chocolates, marshmallow creme and vanilla; set aside.

In a heavy 3-qt (3-l) saucepan over medium-low heat, combine the sugar, condensed milk, water, cream and butter. Stir until the sugar dissolves. Using a pastry brush dipped in water, brush down the sides of the pan to prevent sugar crystals from forming. Raise the heat to high and bring the mixture to a rolling boil. Reduce the heat to medium-high and clip a candy thermometer onto the pan. Using a wooden spoon, stir constantly but slowly until it reaches 232°F (111°C), about 9 minutes.

Pour the boiling mixture all at once over the chocolate in the metal bowl; do not scrape the syrupy residue from the pan bottom. Stir vigorously with a wooden spoon until the chocolate melts and the fudge thickens slightly, about 2 minutes. Stir in the nut mixture. Immediately pour the fudge into the prepared pan and smooth with a rubber spatula. Immediately press the walnut halves into the surface, spacing evenly. Refrigerate uncovered until firm enough to cut, about 1 hour.

Using the foil overhang as an aid, lift the fudge from the pan. Peel the foil from the sides. Trim the edges of the fudge evenly and cut into 32 pieces. Store in an airtight container in the refrigerator for up to 2 weeks. Serve at room temperature.

Makes 32 pieces

Pecan-Molasses Toffee

1¼ cups (10 oz/315 g) unsalted butter

1 cup (8 oz/250 g) granulated sugar

¼ cup (2 oz/60 g) firmly packed golden brown sugar

¼ cup (2 fl oz/60 ml) water

1 tablespoon dark molasses

1 cup (4 oz/125 g) very coarsely chopped pecans, plus ½ cup (2 oz/60 g) medium-fine chopped pecans

½ teaspoon ground cinnamon

6 oz (185 g) bittersweet or semisweet chocolate, finely chopped

The molasses gives this candy a deep flavor, the nuts lend great crunch, and the rich chocolate coating provides an elegant finish. Walnuts, almonds or hazelnuts (filberts) can be substituted for the pecans.

*B*utter a small baking sheet. In a heavy 2½-qt (2.5-l) saucepan over low heat, melt the butter. Add the granulated sugar, brown sugar, water and molasses and stir until the sugar dissolves. Raise the heat to medium and clip a candy thermometer onto the side of the pan. Cook, stirring slowly but constantly, until the thermometer registers 290°F (143°C), about 15 minutes.

Remove from the heat. Stir in the 1 cup (4 oz/125 g) coarsely chopped pecans and the cinnamon. Immediately pour the mixture all at once onto the prepared sheet; do not scrape the residue from the pan bottom. Let stand for 1 minute. Sprinkle the chocolate over the toffee. Let stand for 1 minute to soften. Then, using the back of a metal spoon, spread the chocolate over the toffee until melted. Sprinkle with the ½ cup (2 oz/60 g) medium-fine chopped pecans. Refrigerate uncovered until the candy is firm, about 2 hours.

Break into 2-inch (5-cm) pieces. Store in an airtight container in the refrigerator for up to 3 weeks.

Makes about 1½ lb (750 g)

Maple-Nut Pralines

2 cups (16 fl oz/500 ml) pure maple
   syrup
1 cup (8 fl oz/250 ml) heavy (double)
   cream, plus 2 tablespoons if needed
1 tablespoon unsalted butter
1 cup (4 oz/125 g) walnuts, chopped
1 cup (4 oz/125 g) pecans, chopped
½ teaspoon ground nutmeg

New Orleans–style candies enriched with the New England accent of pure maple syrup. Stacked on a plate or piled in a decorated canister, they make a wonderful hostess gift.

*O*il 2 baking sheets. In a heavy saucepan over medium heat, stir together the maple syrup and the 1 cup (8 fl oz/ 250 ml) cream. Clip a candy thermometer onto the side of the pan. Boil until the thermometer registers 238°F (114°C), about 15 minutes.

Remove from the heat and let cool to 220°F (104°C), about 5 minutes.

Add the butter and stir just until melted and the mixture is creamy, about 1 minute. Stir in the walnuts, pecans and nutmeg. Immediately, using a tablespoon, scoop up spoonfuls of the mixture and drop onto the prepared baking sheets, spacing evenly. (If the mixture becomes too dry to drop, add 2 tablespoons cream and stir over low heat until melted.)

Let cool completely. Store in an airtight container at room temperature for up to 3 weeks.

Makes about 2½ dozen

Macadamia and Coconut Clusters

10 oz (315 g) milk chocolate, preferably European, chopped

3 oz (90 g) bittersweet or semisweet chocolate, chopped

2 cups (10 oz/315 g) coarsely chopped lightly salted roasted macadamia nuts

1½ cups (6 oz/185 g) sweetened shredded coconut, lightly toasted

Easy-to-make gift treats with a delightful taste of the tropics. You can vary the ratio of milk chocolate and bittersweet chocolate if you like, or use only one or the other. Place the individual pieces in paper candy cups for gift giving.

Line a baking sheet with parchment paper or waxed paper.

Place both chocolates in the top pan of a double boiler or in a heatproof bowl. Set over (but not touching) hot (not simmering) water. Heat, stirring constantly, until melted and smooth.

Pour out the hot water from the bottom pan and replace it with lukewarm water. Replace the top pan or heatproof bowl. Let the chocolate stand uncovered, stirring frequently, until it cools slightly and begins to thicken, about 10 minutes.

Stir the macadamia nuts and coconut into the chocolate, mixing thoroughly. Using a small spoon, scoop out slightly rounded teaspoonfuls of the mixture and drop onto the prepared sheet, spacing evenly. Refrigerate uncovered until set, about 2 hours.

Store in an airtight container in the refrigerator for up to 1 month or in the freezer for up to 2 months.

Makes about 4 dozen

Cranberry-Almond Biscotti

1 cup (4 oz/125 g) dried cranberries

2 eggs

¾ cup (6 oz/185 g) granulated sugar, plus extra for topping

½ cup (4 fl oz/125 ml) vegetable oil

2 tablespoons finely grated orange zest

1 teaspoon ground cinnamon

1¼ teaspoons baking powder

1 teaspoon vanilla extract (essence)

½ teaspoon almond extract (essence)

¼ teaspoon salt

2 cups (10 oz/315 g) all-purpose (plain) flour, or as needed

1 cup (4½ oz/140 g) slivered blanched almonds

These festive cookies are perfect for any occasion. They look great when presented in a glass jar, or in a twist-tie-sealed plastic bag tucked inside a pretty gift bag. Try topping them with chocolate coating (recipe on page 8) or confectioners' sugar icing (page 9).

✳

Preheat an oven to 350°F (180°C). Place the cranberries in a bowl with hot water to cover and let stand for 10 minutes. Drain and set aside.

In a large bowl, combine the eggs, the ¾ cup (6 oz/185 g) sugar, oil, orange zest, cinnamon, baking powder, vanilla extract, almond extract and salt. Whisk to blend. Add the flour, almonds and cranberries and stir until a dough forms. Turn out onto a heavily floured surface and knead until smooth, adding more flour if too sticky to work, about 20 turns. Divide the dough in half.

Continuing to work on the floured surface, form each half into a log 2 inches (5 cm) in diameter. Carefully transfer the logs to an ungreased baking sheet, spacing them well apart. Sprinkle the tops with sugar.

Bake until golden brown and firm to the touch, about 30 minutes. Let cool for 10 minutes. Leave the oven set at 350°F.

Using a spatula, carefully transfer the logs to a work surface. Using a serrated knife, cut on the diagonal into slices ½ inch (12 mm) thick. Return the slices cut-side down to the baking sheet. Bake until brown, about 20 minutes.

Transfer the cookies to wire racks to cool. Store in an airtight container at room temperature for up to 2 weeks.

Makes about 3 dozen

Holiday Orange-Spice Cutouts

½ cup (2½ oz/75 g) slivered almonds

2 cups (10 oz/315 g) all-purpose (plain) flour

¾ cup (6 oz/185 g) firmly packed dark brown sugar

2 teaspoons ground ginger

1½ teaspoons ground cinnamon

1 teaspoon ground cloves

½ teaspoon salt

½ teaspoon baking soda (bicarbonate of soda)

¼ cup (2 oz/60 g) unsalted butter, at room temperature

¼ cup (2 oz/60 g) vegetable shortening

¼ cup (2 fl oz/60 ml) dark molasses

1 egg

1 tablespoon finely grated orange zest

colored sugar crystals, optional

confectioners' sugar icing (*recipe on page 9*), optional

For decorating the holiday tree or wreath, cut a hole in each cookie before baking, then thread with ribbons when baked.

❋

*I*n a food processor fitted with the metal blade or in a blender, pulse to grind the almonds finely (do not grind to a paste). Add ¼ cup (1½ oz/45 g) of the flour and ¼ cup (2 oz/60 g) of the brown sugar and grind to a powder; set aside.

In a bowl, sift together the remaining 1¾ cups (8½ oz/270 g) flour, the ginger, cinnamon, cloves, salt and baking soda; set aside. In a large bowl, combine the butter, shortening and the remaining ½ cup (4 oz/125 g) brown sugar. Using an electric mixer set on high speed, beat until light and fluffy. Add the molasses, egg and orange zest and beat until light and fluffy. Add the flour mixture and nut mixture and beat on low speed just until incorporated. Gather into a ball, then divide in half. Form each half into a flat disk. Wrap separately in waxed paper and chill until firm, at least 1 hour or as long as overnight.

Preheat an oven to 350°F (180°C). Generously butter baking sheets. Flour 1 disk and place between 2 sheets of waxed paper. Roll out ¼ inch (6 mm) thick. Using decoratively shaped cookie cutters, cut out cookies. Transfer to the prepared sheets, spacing them ½ inch (12 mm) apart. Sprinkle with sugar crystals, if desired. Pat the scraps into a disk and chill.

Bake until firm on the edges and brown on the bottom, about 10 minutes. Transfer to wire racks to cool. Repeat with the remaining dough disk and dough scraps.

If you have not used sugar crystals, top the cooled cookies with confectioners' sugar icing, if desired. Store in an airtight container at room temperature for up to 3 weeks.

Makes about 3½ dozen 3-inch (7.5-cm) cookies

Chocolate, Nut and Fig Panforte

1½ cups (8 oz/250 g) whole almonds, toasted

1 cup (5 oz/155 g) pine nuts, toasted

1½ cups (8 oz/250 g) chopped, stemmed dried Calimyrna figs

1½ cups (9 oz/280 g) golden raisins

1 cup (6 oz/185 g) diced candied orange peel

¾ cup (4 oz/125 g) unbleached all-purpose (plain) flour

¾ cup (2½ oz/75 g) unsweetened cocoa powder, preferably Dutch process, plus extra for topping

1 tablespoon finely grated lemon zest

1½ teaspoons ground cinnamon

1 teaspoon ground allspice

¾ teaspoon ground coriander

1¼ cups (10 oz/315 g) granulated sugar

1¼ cups (15 oz/470 g) honey

3 tablespoons unsalted butter

4 oz (125 g) semisweet chocolate, finely chopped

Panforte is a chewy, fruit-and-nut Christmas confection from Siena, Italy. Because it is very dense, serve in small pieces.

✳

Preheat an oven to 300°F (150°C). Generously butter two 8-inch (20-cm) cake pans with removable bottoms. Line the pan bottoms with parchment paper or waxed paper. Brush the paper generously with melted butter.

In a large bowl, stir together the almonds, pine nuts, figs, raisins, orange peel, flour, the ¾ cup (2½ oz/75 g) cocoa powder, lemon zest, cinnamon, allspice and coriander. Set aside.

In a heavy saucepan over medium-high heat, combine the sugar, honey and butter. Stir with a wooden spoon until the butter melts and the sugar dissolves. Bring to a rolling boil. Clip a candy thermometer onto the pan. Boil until it registers 238°F (114°C), about 4 minutes. Immediately pour over the nut mixture. Stir quickly to combine, then immediately divide between the prepared pans. Using the back of a spoon, spread evenly.

Bake until the edges begin to brown and the tops appear dry, about 1 hour. Cool in the pans on wire racks for 10 minutes.

Cut out two 8-inch (20-cm) cardboard rounds. Run a small sharp knife around the pan edges to loosen the cakes. Turn out onto the rounds. Peel off the parchment or waxed paper.

Place the chocolate in the top pan of a double boiler or in a heatproof bowl. Set over (but not touching) simmering water and heat, stirring constantly, until melted and smooth. Spread half of the chocolate over each cake. Refrigerate uncovered until the chocolate is set, about 1 hour.

Dust the tops with cocoa. Store tightly wrapped at cool room temperature for up to 1 month.

Makes two 8-inch (20-cm) cakes

Vanilla and Walnut Shortbread Hearts

1 cup (5 oz/155 g) all-purpose (plain) flour

2½ tablespoons cornstarch

⅛ teaspoon salt

½ cup (4 oz/125 g) unsalted butter, at room temperature

⅓ cup (3 oz/90 g) granulated sugar

1 teaspoon vanilla extract (essence)

½ cup (2 oz/60 g) walnuts, finely chopped

This festive cookie looks pretty whether left plain, sprinkled with colored sugar crystals, or decorated with confectioners' sugar icing (recipe on page 9) or chocolate coating (page 8). If using the latter, store the cookies in the refrigerator.

❈

*P*reheat an oven to 350°F (180°C).

In a bowl, sift together the flour, cornstarch and salt; set aside. In a large bowl, combine the butter, sugar and vanilla. Using an electric mixer set on high, beat until light and fluffy. Reduce the speed to low, add the flour mixture and mix until beginning to gather together into a rough dough. Mix in the walnuts.

Turn out the dough onto a sheet of waxed paper. Gather into a ball, then flatten into a disk. Cover with another sheet of waxed paper. Roll out the dough ¼ inch (6 mm) thick. Remove the top sheet of waxed paper and, using a heart-shaped cookie cutter 3 inches (7.5 cm) in diameter, cut out cookies. Transfer the cookies to an ungreased baking sheet, spacing them ½ inch (12 mm) apart. Gather up the scraps into a flat disk, reroll and cut out additional cookies. Transfer to the baking sheet.

Bake until firm to the touch and just beginning to color, about 20 minutes. Transfer the cookies to wire racks to cool. Store in an airtight container at room temperature for up to 2 weeks.

Makes about 20

Triple-Chocolate Brownies

4 oz (125 g) unsweetened chocolate, chopped
½ cup (4 oz/125 g) unsalted butter
1¼ cups (10 oz/315 g) granulated sugar
1 teaspoon vanilla extract (essence)
¼ teaspoon salt
3 eggs
¾ cup (4 oz/125 g) all-purpose (plain) flour
⅔ cup (3 oz/90 g) chopped walnuts
½ cup (3 oz/90 g) milk chocolate chips
½ cup (3 oz/90 g) white chocolate chips

A batch of bittersweet brownies accented with milk chocolate and white chocolate chips is the perfect gift for a chocolate lover.

Preheat an oven to 325°F (165°C). Line an 8-inch (20-cm) square baking pan with aluminum foil, allowing the foil to overhang the sides slightly.

In a large, heavy saucepan over low heat, combine the unsweetened chocolate and butter. Stir until melted and smooth. Let cool slightly.

Whisk the sugar, vanilla and salt into the chocolate mixture. One at a time, whisk in the eggs, mixing well after each addition, then continue to whisk until the mixture is velvety, about 2 minutes. Add the flour and whisk just until blended. Stir in the walnuts and the milk chocolate and white chocolate chips. Pour the batter into the prepared pan and smooth the surface.

Bake until the top is just springy to the touch and a toothpick inserted in the center comes out with a few moist crumbs attached, about 40 minutes. Let cool in the pan on a wire rack.

Using the foil, lift the sheet of brownies from the pan and place on a work surface. Peel the foil off the sides. Cut into 16 squares. Store in an airtight container in the refrigerator for up to 4 days.

Makes 16

Fennel, Parmesan and Pepper Breadsticks

about 3½ cups (17½ oz/545 g)
   unbleached all-purpose (plain) flour
1 package (2 teaspoons) quick-rise yeast
1 tablespoon granulated sugar
1½ teaspoons salt
1½ teaspoons ground pepper, plus
   extra for sprinkling
1 tablespoon fennel seeds
1¼ cups (10 fl oz/310 ml) hot water
   (125°–130°F/52°–54°C)
2 tablespoons olive oil, plus extra for
   brushing on dough
1 cup (4 oz/125 g) freshly grated
   Parmesan cheese
cornmeal for baking sheet

For a tasty variation, replace the fennel seeds with dried rosemary.

✳

Preheat an oven to 425°F (220°C).

In a large bowl, stir together 2 cups (10 oz/315 g) of the flour, the yeast, sugar, salt and the 1½ teaspoons pepper. In a mortar, lightly crush the fennel seeds. Add to the bowl. Add the hot water and 2 tablespoons oil and stir until smooth. Slowly mix in enough of the remaining 1½ cups (7½ oz/230 g) flour to form a soft dough. Knead on a lightly floured surface, adding flour if the dough is sticky, until smooth and elastic, about 8 minutes. Sprinkle the cheese on the surface and knead it into the dough.

Lightly flour a work surface and transfer the dough to it. Shape into a 4-by-14-inch (10-by-35-cm) rectangle. Brush with olive oil. Cover with plastic wrap and let stand for 10 minutes.

Oil 2 large baking sheets, then sprinkle with cornmeal. Generously sprinkle the dough with additional pepper. Cut the dough crosswise into 4 equal pieces. Cutting in the same direction, cut each piece into 5 smaller pieces. Grasping each end of 1 piece, stretch it until it is 12 inches (30 cm) long. Roll it between your palms and the work surface to smooth the shape. Transfer to the prepared pan. Repeat with the remaining dough pieces, spacing them 1 inch (2.5 cm) apart. Let stand for 15 minutes.

Bake until golden brown, about 15 minutes. Cool on the baking sheets for 15 minutes. For crisp breadsticks, reduce the oven temperature to 300°F (150°C) and bake the cooled breadsticks about 15 minutes longer. Cool on a wire rack. Wrap tightly and store at room temperature for up to 2 days.

Makes 20

Currant, Lemon and Ginger Cake

1½ cups (7½ oz/235 g) unbleached all-purpose (plain) flour
1 teaspoon ground cinnamon
1 teaspoon ground ginger
½ teaspoon baking soda (bicarbonate of soda)
1½ cups (9 oz/280 g) dried currants
½ cup (1 oz/30 g) chopped crystallized ginger
¾ cup (6 oz/185 g) plus 2 tablespoons unsalted butter, at room temperature
¾ cup (6 oz/185 g) granulated sugar
3 eggs
2½ teaspoons finely grated lemon zest
¼ cup (2 fl oz/60 ml) fresh lemon juice
confectioners' (icing) sugar for topping

The lively flavors have time to develop if the cake is made a day ahead. Spread it with lemon glaze (recipe on page 8) for a special touch. The cake can be tightly wrapped and stored at room temperature for up to 3 days.

Position a rack in the lower third of an oven and preheat the oven to 350°F (180°C). Butter and flour a 7-cup (56-fl oz/1.75-l) tube pan or bundt pan.

In a bowl, sift together the flour, cinnamon, ground ginger and baking soda. Stir in the currants and crystallized ginger. Set aside.

Place the butter and granulated sugar in a large bowl. Using an electric mixer set on high speed, beat until light and fluffy. Add the eggs, one at a time, beating well after each addition. Mix in the lemon zest. Reduce the speed to low, add the flour mixture and lemon juice and mix just until well combined. Pour the batter into the pan, spreading evenly.

Bake until a toothpick inserted near the center comes out clean, about 50 minutes. Cool the cake in the pan on a wire rack for 20 minutes. Invert onto the rack and let cool completely. Wrap tightly with foil and let mellow overnight at room temperature.

Sift confectioners' sugar over the top before serving.

Makes one 8-inch (20-cm) cake

Chocolate-Walnut Biscotti

4 oz (125 g) semisweet chocolate, coarsely chopped

1 cup (8 oz/250 g) granulated sugar

1¾ cups (9 oz/280 g) all-purpose (plain) flour

⅓ cup (1 oz/30 g) unsweetened cocoa powder

1 teaspoon baking soda (bicarbonate of soda)

¼ teaspoon salt

3 eggs

1 teaspoon vanilla extract (essence)

2½ cups (10 oz/315 g) coarsely chopped walnuts

These flavorful, sophisticated, nut-studded cookies are even better dipped in chocolate coating (recipe on page 8).

❈

Preheat an oven to 300°F (150°C). Line a large baking sheet with parchment paper or waxed paper.

In a food processor fitted with the metal blade, combine the chocolate and sugar and grind until the chocolate is very fine. Set aside. In a bowl, sift together the flour, cocoa powder, baking soda and salt. Set aside.

In the bowl of a heavy-duty mixer, combine the eggs and vanilla. Beat at medium speed to blend. Reduce the speed to low, add the chocolate and flour mixtures and mix until a stiff dough forms, adding the walnuts when about half mixed. Transfer the dough to a floured surface and gather it together. Divide in half. Form each half into a log 12 inches (30 cm) long.

Carefully transfer the logs to the prepared baking sheet, spacing them evenly. Pat to even up the shapes. Bake until almost firm to the touch, about 50 minutes. Let cool for 10 minutes. Leave the oven set at 300°F (150°C).

Using a spatula, transfer the logs to a work surface. Using a serrated knife, cut on the diagonal into slices ½–¾ inch (12 mm–2 cm) thick. Return the slices cut-side down to the baking sheet. Bake for 25 minutes. Turn the slices over and bake until crisp and dry, about 25 minutes longer.

Transfer the cookies to wire racks to cool. Store in an airtight container at room temperature for up to 1 month.

Makes about 2½ dozen

Miniature Chocolate Chip and Coconut Cakes

2 cups (12 oz/375 g) semisweet
  chocolate chips
1½ cups (5 oz/155 g) toasted flaked
  coconut
3 cups (15 oz/470 g) all-purpose
  (plain) flour
2 teaspoons baking soda (bicarbonate
  of soda)
1 teaspoon baking powder
1 teaspoon ground cinnamon
¾ teaspoon salt
1 cup (8 oz/250 g) unsalted butter, at
  room temperature
1½ cups (10½ oz/330 g) firmly packed
  golden brown sugar
4 eggs
2 tablespoons finely grated orange zest
2½ teaspoons vanilla extract (essence)
1 cup (8 fl oz/250 ml) buttermilk
lemon glaze (*recipe on page 8*)

The recipe yields six miniature cakes for six lucky friends.
Of course, you could make one large cake instead.

✻

Preheat an oven to 350°F (180°C). Generously butter
6 miniature loaf pans measuring 3¼ by 5¾ by 2 inches
(8 cm by 14½ cm by 5 cm) or one 9- or 10-cup (72–80 fl
oz/2.25–2.5 l) fluted tube pan; dust with flour.

In a bowl, stir together the chocolate chips, coconut and
2 tablespoons of the flour; set aside. In another bowl, sift
together the remaining flour, baking soda, baking powder,
cinnamon and salt; set aside.

In a large bowl and using an electric mixer set on high
speed, beat the butter until light. Add the brown sugar and
beat until fluffy. Beat in the eggs, one at a time, beating well
after each addition. Beat in the orange zest and vanilla. Then
mix in the flour mixture alternately with the buttermilk, in
3 additions each. Fold in the chocolate chip mixture.

Divide the batter evenly among the prepared pans or
pour into the single pan. Bake until the cake(s) are springy
to the touch and begin to pull away from the sides of the
pan(s), about 45 minutes for mini loaves and 55 minutes
for 1 large cake. Cool in the pan(s) on a wire rack for
15 minutes. Invert onto the rack and let cool completely.

Wrap tightly and store at room temperature for up to
3 days. Just before presenting, spread with the lemon
glaze. For a thicker coating, wait 5 minutes, then spread
with more glaze.

Makes 6 small cakes or 1 large cake

Hazelnut Amaretti

1¼ cups (6½ oz/200 g) hazelnuts
  (filberts)
¾ cup (3 oz/90 g) plus 3 tablespoons
  confectioners' (icing) sugar
1 teaspoon all-purpose (plain) flour
2 egg whites
⅓ cup (3 oz/90 g) granulated sugar
¾ teaspoon almond extract (essence)
pearl sugar for topping, optional

A recipe inspired by the outstanding almond amaretti in Carol Field's The Italian Baker. *The pearl sugar used to top the cookies is available at specialty-food stores, but coarsely crushed sugar cubes work well, too. Wrap each cookie in tissue paper, twist the ends and pack in cookie tins or boxes.*

✴

Preheat an oven to 300°F (150°C). Line a large baking sheet with parchment paper or waxed paper.

In a food processor fitted with the metal blade, finely grind the hazelnuts (do not grind to a paste). Add ¼ cup (1 oz/30 g) of the confectioners' sugar and grind to a powder. Mix in the remaining ½ cup (2 oz/60 g) plus 3 tablespoons confectioners' sugar and the flour. Set aside.

In a bowl, beat the egg whites until soft peaks form. Gradually add the granulated sugar and beat until stiff, shiny peaks form. Fold in the almond extract and the nut mixture.

Spoon the batter into a pastry bag fitted with a ½-inch (12-mm) plain tip. Pipe the batter onto the prepared baking sheet in mounds 1½ inches (4 cm) in diameter. Using a wet finger, smooth the top of each cookie. Sprinkle with pearl sugar, if desired.

Bake until just beginning to brown, about 45 minutes. Turn off the oven, leave the oven door closed and let the cookies dry for 30 minutes.

Transfer the cookies to wire racks to cool completely. Store in an airtight container at room temperature for up to 1 month.

Makes about 3 dozen

Fancy Chocolate Chunk–Oatmeal Cookies

1 cup (5 oz/155 g) all-purpose (plain)
   flour
½ teaspoon ground cinnamon
½ teaspoon baking powder
¼ teaspoon salt
1 cup (8 oz/250 g) unsalted butter, at
   room temperature
1 cup (7 oz/220 g) firmly packed
   golden brown sugar
1 egg
1 tablespoon finely grated orange zest
1 teaspoon vanilla extract (essence)
3 cups (9 oz/280 g) rolled oats
1 cup (4 oz/125 g) chopped walnuts
6 oz (185 g) bittersweet or semisweet
   chocolate, chopped, or 1 cup (6 oz/
   185 g) semisweet chocolate chips

To make the cookies extra special, top them with confectioners' sugar icing (recipe on page 9).

Preheat an oven to 350°F (180°C). Butter baking sheets.

In a bowl, sift together the flour, cinnamon, baking powder and salt; set aside.

Place the butter and brown sugar in a large bowl. Using an electric mixer set on high speed, beat until light and fluffy. Add the egg, orange zest and vanilla and again beat until light and fluffy. Reduce the speed to low, add the flour mixture and beat until well mixed. Beat in the oats, walnuts and chocolate.

Using a tablespoon, scoop up the batter by rounded spoonfuls and shape into balls. Arrange on the prepared baking sheets, spacing 2 inches (5 cm) apart.

Bake until golden brown, about 17 minutes. Transfer the cookies to wire racks to cool completely.

Store in an airtight container at room temperature for up to 1 week.

Makes about 3 dozen

Fig and Walnut Pumpkin Bread

2 cups (14 oz/440 g) firmly packed golden brown sugar

1½ cups (12 oz/375 g) canned solid-pack pumpkin purée

½ cup (4 fl oz/125 ml) vegetable oil

2 eggs

2 teaspoons baking soda (bicarbonate of soda)

½ teaspoon ground cinnamon

½ teaspoon ground ginger

½ teaspoon ground allspice

½ teaspoon salt

1 cup (4 oz/125 g) walnuts, chopped

8 oz (250 g) dried Calimyrna figs, stemmed and chopped (about 1½ cups)

2½ cups (12½ oz/390 g) all-purpose (plain) flour

A wonderfully simple recipe that yields a top-notch fruit cake when 2 cups (10 oz/315 g) chopped mixed dried fruits such as raisins, dates and apricots are added with the figs; baking will take a few minutes longer. For a pretty shine, spread with lemon glaze (recipe on page 8) just before presenting.

✳

Preheat an oven to 350°F (180°C). Butter and flour two 4½-by-8½-by-2½-inch (12-by-22-by-6-cm) loaf pans.

In a large bowl and using a spoon, stir together the brown sugar, pumpkin purée, oil, eggs, baking soda, cinnamon, ginger, allspice and salt until well blended. Stir in the walnuts and figs. Add the flour and stir just until blended. Divide the batter evenly between the prepared pans.

Bake until a toothpick inserted in the center comes out clean, about 55 minutes. Cool the loaves in their pans on wire racks for 10 minutes, then turn out onto the racks and let cool completely.

To store, wrap tightly in aluminum foil. Refrigerate for up to 3 days or freeze for up to 1 month.

Makes 2 loaves

Raisin, Cherry and Apricot Panettone

about 3½ cups (17½ oz/545 g)
   all-purpose (plain) flour
⅓ cup (3 oz/90 g) granulated sugar
1 tablespoon (¼ oz/7 g) active dry yeast
1¼ teaspoons salt
1 cup (8 fl oz/250 ml) milk
½ cup (4 oz/125 g) butter
¼ cup (3 oz/90 g) honey
2 tablespoons finely grated orange zest
1 tablespoon finely grated lemon zest
2 eggs
½ teaspoon vanilla extract (essence)
¾ cup (4½ oz/140 g) golden raisins
¾ cup (3 oz/90 g) pitted dried sour or
   Bing cherries
¾ cup (4½ oz/140 g) diced dried
   apricots
1 egg beaten with 1 tablespoon water
   for glaze

Use a panettone pan or coffee cans or charlotte molds for baking this festive Milanese bread.

*In a large bowl, stir together 1½ cups (7½ oz/235 g) of the flour, the sugar, yeast and salt. Set aside. In a small saucepan, combine the milk, butter, honey, and orange and lemon zests. Heat, stirring frequently, until a candy thermometer registers 125°–130°F (52°–54°C). Using an electric mixer set on medium speed, gradually beat the hot liquid into the flour mixture. Beat for 2 minutes. Add the eggs, vanilla and ½ cup (2½ oz/75 g) of the remaining flour; beat on high speed 2 minutes longer. Stir in enough of the remaining 1½ cups (7½ oz/235 g) flour to form a stiff batter. Cover with plastic wrap and let rise in a warm, draft-free area until doubled, about 1¼ hours.

Generously butter two 1-lb (500-g) coffee cans or other 1-qt (1-l) molds, or one 2-qt (2-l) mold or pan. Line the bottoms with parchment paper and brush the paper with melted butter.

Stir down the batter, then mix in the raisins, cherries and apricots. Pour into the mold(s). Cut a deep X in the top(s). Cover and let rise in a warm area until almost doubled, about 1 hour.

Position the rack in the lowest third of an oven and preheat to 350°F (180°C). Recut the X in the top of the bread(s). Brush the bread(s) with the egg glaze. Bake until golden brown and a toothpick inserted in the center comes out clean, about 45 minutes for 2 small loaves and 55 minutes for 1 large loaf.

Cool in the mold(s) on a rack for 5 minutes. Unmold and remove paper. Place the bread(s) on their sides on the rack to cool. Store tightly wrapped at room temperature for up to 2 days.

Makes 1 large or 2 small loaves

Scones with Chocolate Chips and Dried Cherries

2 cups (10 oz/315 g) all-purpose (plain) flour

¼ cup (2 oz/60 g) granulated sugar, plus extra for topping

1 tablespoon baking powder

½ teaspoon ground cinnamon

¼ teaspoon salt

¾ cup (3 oz/90 g) coarsely chopped dried pitted sour cherries

½ cup (3 oz/90 g) miniature semisweet chocolate chips

1⅓ cups (11 fl oz/330 ml) heavy (double) cream, or as needed

melted butter

These are a welcome addition to any breakfast or tea party. Dried cranberries or golden raisins can replace the cherries.

❄

*P*reheat an oven to 425°F (220°C).

In a large bowl, sift together the flour, the ¼ cup (2 oz/ 60 g) sugar, baking powder, cinnamon and salt. Stir in the cherries and chocolate chips. Using a fork, stir in enough cream to form a slightly moist dough. Gather the dough into a ball.

Transfer the dough to a floured work surface and knead gently until smooth, about 15 turns. Add more cream if necessary to moisten the dough. Roll out the dough ¾ inch (2 cm) thick. Using a floured biscuit cutter or glass 2½ inches (6 cm) in diameter, cut out rounds. Transfer the rounds to an ungreased baking sheet. Gather together the scraps, pat out ¾ inch (2 cm) thick and cut out additional scones. Add to the baking sheet.

Brush the scones with melted butter. Sprinkle with sugar. Bake until light brown and just firm to the touch, about 20 minutes.

Serve warm, or let cool on racks and serve at room temperature. To store, wrap tightly in aluminum foil and keep at room temperature for up to 1 day.

Makes about 1 dozen

Orange and Rosemary Vinegar

2 fresh rosemary sprigs
about 1½ cups (12 fl oz/375 ml) red
   wine vinegar
3 orange zest strips, each 2 inches
   (5 cm) long and 1 inch (2.5 cm) wide

Easy, attractive and delicious. Select an interesting bottle, add a bottle of your favorite olive oil and you have a wonderful gift. Mix them together to make an outstanding vinaigrette for fresh greens and vegetables.

Wash a 1½-cup (12-fl oz/375-ml) bottle in hot soapy water; rinse well. Fill the bottle with hot water.

Meanwhile, rinse the rosemary sprigs and pat dry. In a small saucepan over medium heat, warm the vinegar until it is hot.

Drain the bottle well. While the bottle is still hot, place the rosemary and orange zest in it. Pour in the hot vinegar. Cover tightly and let stand at room temperature for 2 weeks to allow the flavors to blend. Keeps indefinitely at room temperature.

Makes about 1½ cups (12 fl oz/375 ml)

Roasted Bell Peppers in Flavored Oil

1 large red bell pepper (capsicum)
1 large yellow bell pepper (capsicum)
2 teaspoons chopped fresh rosemary
2 teaspoons chopped fresh thyme
ground black pepper
8 thin lemon slices
¾ cup (6 fl oz/180 ml) extra-virgin
   olive oil, or as needed
1 small dried red chili pepper

The alternating layers of red and yellow peppers are especially attractive in a glass jar. This makes a delicious antipasto, served with Italian bread.

Using a fork, hold the bell peppers directly over a gas flame on a stove top and turn occasionally until evenly blackened and blistered on all sides. Alternatively, preheat a broiler (griller). Place the bell peppers on a broiler pan and broil (grill), turning occasionally, until evenly blackened and blistered.

Transfer the peppers to a closed paper bag and let stand for 10 minutes. Using your fingers, carefully peel off the blackened skins, then remove the stems, ribs and seeds and discard. Cut the peppers lengthwise into strips ½ inch (12 mm) wide.

Layer half of the red pepper slices in a 1-pint (16-fl oz/500-ml) jar with a lid. Sprinkle with ½ teaspoon each rosemary and thyme and then with black pepper. Top with 2 lemon slices. Layer half of the yellow pepper slices and sprinkle with ½ teaspoon each rosemary and thyme and then black pepper. Top with 2 lemon slices. Repeat the layering. Add enough olive oil to cover the peppers. Top with the dried chili pepper.

Cover and store in the refrigerator for at least 1 day to allow the flavors to blend. Keeps refrigerated for up to 2 weeks.

Makes about 1 pint (16 fl oz/500 ml)

Peach Vinegar

3 small, ripe peaches, pitted and
   coarsely chopped (unpeeled)
1 cinnamon stick, about 3 inches
   (7.5 cm) long, broken into pieces
1½ cups (12 fl oz/375 ml) Champagne
   vinegar or white wine vinegar, or
   as needed

*Fresh summer fruit and cinnamon add a lovely pale peach color
and an intriguing aroma to this delicate vinegar. Pair it with
hazelnut or walnut oil and toss with young, tender greens.*

Wash two 1-pint (16-fl oz/500-ml) jars in hot soapy
water; rinse well. Drain and wipe dry.

Divide the peaches and cinnamon between the jars. Add
enough vinegar to each jar to submerge the peaches
completely. Cover and refrigerate for 2 weeks.

Wash 1 or 2 bottles in hot soapy water; rinse well. Drain
thoroughly. Strain the vinegar through a fine-mesh sieve,
and then through a coffee filter. Pour the vinegar into the
bottle(s). Cover tightly and store at room temperature.
Keeps for up to 2 months.

Makes about 1½ cups (12 fl oz/375 ml)

Hot Spiced Cider Sachets

6 cinnamon sticks, each about 3 inches (7.5 cm) long

30 whole cardamom pods

30 whole cloves

18 crystallized ginger slices, each about 1 inch (2.5 cm) in diameter

12 small bay leaves

Nothing tastes better than hot cider on a cold winter's day. Present these sachets with a gift card that reads: To make great spiced cider, simmer 2 quarts (2 l) cider with 1 sachet in a covered pan for 30 minutes. Ladle into mugs and enjoy. Sweeten to taste. These aromatic sachets can be also used for making mulled wine; simply substitute red wine for the cider.

Cut out six 5-inch (13-cm) squares of cheesecloth (muslin). Break the cinnamon sticks into pieces and divide them evenly among the squares. Place 5 cardamom pods, 5 cloves, 3 ginger slices and 2 bay leaves atop each square. Bring the corners of each square together and tie with kitchen string, white thread or twine. Use immediately, or place in an airtight container and store at room temperature for up to 2 months.

Makes 6

Olives with Orange and Fennel

8 oz (250 g) imported black olives such
   as Kalamata
1 teaspoon fennel seeds
3 orange zest strips, each 2 inches
   (5 cm) long by 1 inch (2.5 cm) wide
2 large bay leaves, preferably California
¾ cup (6 fl oz/180 ml) olive oil, or as
   needed

An attractive, easy-to-make appetizer that adds an unusual touch to any hors-d'oeuvre tray. Make gifts of them by placing in glass jars or ceramic crocks. A good selection of brine-cured olives can be found at Mediterranean delicatessens.

*P*at the olives dry. Place on a firm work surface and, using the side of a large knife, crush each olive just until the skin cracks. Place in a container with a tight-fitting cover.

Lightly crush the fennel seeds in a mortar with a pestle. Add to the olives, along with the orange zest strips and bay leaves. Add enough olive oil to cover the olives. Let stand for 4 hours at room temperature.

Cover and refrigerate for at least 2 days to allow the flavors to blend. Keeps refrigerated for up to 2 months. Serve at room temperature.

Makes about 2 cups (10 oz/315 g)

Olive Oil with Lemon and Bay Leaf

1 large fresh lemon
1 cup (8 fl oz/250 ml) extra-virgin
  olive oil
1 bay leaf, preferably California
¼ teaspoon whole peppercorns

Flavored oils have many uses. Include a gift tag suggesting brushing this on toasted Italian bread, mixing it with pasta and grated pecorino romano cheese, or tossing it with a salad. Use the highly aromatic California bay leaves in this recipe if you can.

Scrub the lemon with an abrasive sponge to remove all surface impurities. Rinse thoroughly and dry well.

Pour the olive oil into a small heavy saucepan. Using a zester and working directly over the pan, remove the zest from the lemon, letting it fall into the oil. Add the bay leaf and peppercorns. Clip a candy thermometer onto the side of the pan. Heat the oil over medium-low heat until the thermometer registers 200°F (93°C). Cook at 200°–225°F (93°–107°C) for 10 minutes. Remove from the heat and let cool slightly.

Sterilize a bottle according to the directions on page 10. Transfer the oil mixture to the hot, sterilized bottle. Cover and store at room temperature for up to 2 months.

Makes about 1 cup (8 fl oz/250 ml)

Kitchen Potpourri

¼ cup (2½ oz/75 g) whole cloves
1 cup (1¼ oz/37 g) whole allspice
10 cinnamon sticks, each 3 inches
   (7.5 cm) long, broken into pieces
8 small bay leaves
4 whole nutmegs
3 tablespoons star anise
2 tablespoons whole cardamom pods

The same spices that lend so much character to cooked foods can also be kept around every day to fill the kitchen with a pleasant scent. Place the mixture in an oversized cup, a decorative bowl or a cachepot for setting out on a kitchen counter.

Combine all the ingredients in a bowl, mixing well. Store indefinitely at room temperature, stirring occasionally.

Makes about 2 cups (6 oz/185 g)

Spiced Nuts

2½ cups (10–12 oz/315–375 g) nuts of
  your choice
2 tablespoons vegetable oil
1½ teaspoons ground cumin
¼ teaspoon cayenne pepper
2 tablespoons granulated sugar
1 teaspoon salt

*The recipe calls for using nuts of your choice; try pecans,
almonds, peanuts, walnuts or a mixture. They are best served
hot, so enclose a gift card saying to spread on a baking sheet
and reheat in a 300°F (150°C) oven for about 5 minutes.*

Preheat an oven to 300°F (150°C). Place the nuts in a bowl.
  Pour the oil into a small, heavy saucepan and place over
medium-low heat until warm. Add the cumin and cayenne
and stir until the mixture is aromatic, about 15 seconds.
Pour the flavored oil over the nuts. Add the sugar and salt
and stir to coat evenly. Transfer the nuts to a baking pan.
  Bake, stirring occasionally, until the nuts are toasted,
about 20 minutes.
  Store in an airtight container for up to 2 weeks.

Makes about 2½ cups (10 oz/315 g)

Lemon-Spice Olives

½ lb (250 g) imported large green olives such as French or Spanish
½ small lemon, thinly sliced crosswise
¾ cup (6 fl oz/180 ml) olive oil, or as needed
1 teaspoon dried oregano, crumbled
½ teaspoon red pepper flakes
½ teaspoon ground black pepper

A long-keeping treat, these olives are an ideal offering to drop-in guests. For a doubly good gift, give one crock filled with these and another with the olives with orange and fennel (recipe on page 75).

*P*at the olives dry. Place on a firm work surface and, using the side of a large knife, crush each olive just until the skin cracks. Place in a container with a tight-fitting cover. Add the lemon slices.

In a small saucepan over medium-low heat, combine the ¾ cup (6 fl oz/180 ml) olive oil, oregano, red pepper flakes and black pepper. Bring just to a simmer. Pour over the olives, adding enough oil to cover the olives completely. Let stand for 4 hours at room temperature.

Cover and refrigerate for at least 2 days to allow the flavors to blend. Keeps refrigerated for up to 2 months. Serve at room temperature.

Makes about 2 cups (10 oz/315 g)

Plum-Vanilla Preserves

4 lb (2 kg) plums, preferably purple-
   fleshed Santa Rosa
1 cup (8 fl oz/250 ml) fresh orange juice
½ cup (4 fl oz/125 ml) fresh lemon
   juice
4 whole allspice
2 cinnamon sticks, each about 3 inches
   (7.5 cm) long
7 cups (3½ lb/1.75 kg) granulated sugar
1 vanilla bean, split lengthwise and
   then crosswise

Make these preserves in mid-summer, when plums are at their best.

*H*alve and pit the plums, then cut into slices ½ inch (12 mm) thick. Place in a heavy nonaluminum saucepan and add the orange and lemon juices, allspice and cinnamon. Bring to a boil over high heat. Reduce the heat, cover and simmer, stirring occasionally, until very tender, about 20 minutes.

Add the sugar and vanilla bean and stir until the sugar dissolves. Simmer, uncovered, stirring and crushing the fruit with the back of a wooden spoon occasionally at first and then more frequently near the end of cooking, about 45 minutes longer, until the jelling stage is reached. To test, remove from the heat. Fill a chilled spoon with the preserves, then slowly pour the preserves back into the pan; the last 2 drops should merge and fall from the spoon in a sheet. Alternatively, spoon 1 tablespoon preserves onto a chilled plate and place in the freezer for 2 minutes; it should wrinkle when gently pushed with a fingertip.

Meanwhile, wash four 1-pint (16-fl oz/500-ml) canning jars and lids in hot soapy water; rinse well. Fill the jars with hot water. Place the lids in a small saucepan. Add water to cover and bring to a simmer. Remove from the heat.

Drain 1 jar. Spoon the hot preserves and 1 vanilla bean piece into the jar to within ¼ inch (6 mm) of the top. Using a towel dipped into hot water, immediately wipe the rim clean. Drain 1 lid and place atop the jar; seal tightly with the screw band. Repeat with the remaining preserves and jars.

Following the directions on page 11, process the jars in a hot-water bath, check seals, label and store. (If the preserves will be kept no longer than 3 weeks, omit the water bath and store in the refrigerator.)

Makes about 4 pints (64 fl oz/2 l)

Raspberry–Red Wine Sauce

1 bottle (3 cups/24 fl oz/750 ml) dry
    red wine
1 package (12 oz/375 g) frozen
    unsweetened raspberries
1½ cups (12 oz/375 g) granulated sugar
1 vanilla bean, split lengthwise and
    then crosswise

This elegant, ruby-colored sauce is perfect spooned over vanilla ice cream or a slice of pound cake and garnished with fresh raspberries. Store in fancy jars for gift giving.

In a heavy nonaluminum saucepan over medium heat, combine the wine, berries, sugar and vanilla bean. Stir until the sugar dissolves, then simmer for 10 minutes. Raise the heat to medium-high and boil until the mixture is reduced to 2½ cups (20 fl oz/625 ml), about 30 minutes longer.

Meanwhile, wash canning jars and lids in hot soapy water; rinse well. Fill the jars with hot water. Place the lids in a small saucepan. Add water to cover and bring to a simmer. Remove from the heat.

Pour the berry mixture through a sieve into a bowl, pressing on the berries with the back of a wooden spoon to extract as much pulp as possible. Retrieve the vanilla bean pieces and rinse them. Return the sauce to the pan along with the vanilla bean pieces. Bring to a boil.

Drain 1 jar. Spoon the sauce into the jar to within ¼ inch (6 mm) of the top. Using a towel dipped into hot water, immediately wipe the rim clean. Drain 1 lid and place atop the jar; seal tightly with the screw band. Repeat with the remaining sauce and jars.

Following the directions on page 11, process the jars in a hot-water bath, check seals, label and store. (If the sauce will be kept for no longer than 3 weeks, it is not necessary to use a water bath. Simply store in the refrigerator.)

Makes about 2 cups (16 fl oz/500 ml)

Dried-Fruit Chutney

½ lb (250 g) dried peaches, chopped
½ lb (250 g) dried apricots, chopped
½ lb (250 g) dried Calimyrna figs,
   stems removed and chopped
2 cups (16 fl oz/500 ml) cider vinegar
½ lb (250 g) pitted dates, chopped
½ lb (250 g) pitted prunes, chopped
1 large yellow onion, chopped
1 cup (8 oz/250 g) granulated sugar
1½ teaspoons Madras curry powder
1 teaspoon ground ginger
¼ teaspoon red pepper flakes
¼ teaspoon salt

Using dried fruits means you can make this spicy condiment any time of the year. It's the perfect partner for roasted or grilled meats. If you decide to put the chutney into jars that are not standard canning jars, omit the water bath and store in the refrigerator.

In a bowl, combine the peaches, apricots and figs. Pour in enough hot water to cover and let stand for 30 minutes. Drain, reserving 1¼ cups (10 fl oz/310 ml) of the soaking water.

In a large, heavy nonaluminum saucepan over high heat, combine the soaked fruits, the reserved soaking water, vinegar, dates, prunes, onion, sugar, curry powder, ginger, red pepper flakes and salt. Bring to a boil, stirring until the sugar dissolves. Reduce the heat and simmer, stirring frequently, until the chutney is thick and the fruits are tender, about 10 minutes.

Meanwhile, wash canning jars and lids in hot soapy water; rinse well. Fill the jars with hot water. Place the lids in a small saucepan. Add water to cover and bring to a simmer. Remove from the heat.

Drain 1 jar. Spoon the hot chutney into the jar to within ¼ inch (6 mm) of the top. Run a nonmetallic spatula between the chutney and the jar to remove air bubbles. Using a towel dipped into hot water, immediately wipe the rim clean. Drain 1 lid and place atop the jar; seal tightly with the screw band. Repeat with the remaining chutney and jars.

Following the directions on page 11, process the jars in a hot-water bath, check seals, label and store. (If the chutney will be kept for no longer than 3 weeks, it is not necessary to use a water bath. Simply store in the refrigerator.)

Makes about 3½ pints (56 fl oz/1.75 l)

Peaches-and-Spice Jam

A jam made with everyone's favorite summer fruit.

4 lb (2 kg) peaches
4 cups (2 lb/1 kg) granulated sugar
¼ cup (2 fl oz/60 ml) fresh lemon juice
2 cinnamon sticks, each 3 inches
  (7.5 cm) long
10 whole cardamom pods
4 whole cloves

Have ready a large bowl three-fourths full of cold water. Bring a large saucepan three-fourths full of water to a boil. Add half the peaches and blanch for 30 seconds. Using a slotted spoon, transfer the peaches to the bowl of water. Repeat with the remaining peaches. Drain the peaches, then peel, halve and pit them. Working over a large, heavy nonaluminum saucepan, cut the peaches lengthwise into slices, allowing their juices and the slices to fall into the pan. Stir in the sugar, lemon juice, cinnamon, cardamom and cloves. Let stand for 1 hour.

Place the pan over medium heat and cook, stirring, until the sugar dissolves. Raise the heat and bring to a slow boil. Cook uncovered to the jelling stage, stirring occasionally at first and then more frequently near the end of cooking, about 30 minutes. To test for doneness, remove from the heat. Fill a chilled spoon with the jam, then slowly pour it back into the pan; the last 2 drops should merge and fall in a sheet. Alternatively, spoon 1 tablespoon jam onto a chilled plate and freeze for 2 minutes; it should wrinkle when gently pushed with a fingertip.

Meanwhile, wash canning jars and lids in hot soapy water; rinse well. Fill the jars with hot water. Put the lids in a pan with water to cover and bring to a simmer. Remove from the heat.

Drain 1 jar. Spoon in the hot jam and a few spices to within ¼ inch (6 mm) of the top. Using a hot, damp towel, wipe the rim clean. Drain 1 lid and place on the jar; seal tightly with the screw band. Repeat with the remaining jam and jars. Following the directions on page 11, process the jars in a hot-water bath, check seals, label and store. (If keeping no longer than 3 weeks, omit the water bath and store in the refrigerator.)

Makes about 2½ pints (40 fl oz/1.25 l)

Orange-Lemon Curd

3 eggs

1 cup (8 oz/250 g) granulated sugar

6 tablespoons (3 fl oz/90 ml) strained fresh orange juice

2 tablespoons (1 fl oz/30 ml) strained fresh lemon juice

6 tablespoons (3 oz/90 g) unsalted butter, cut into pieces

3 tablespoons finely grated orange zest

¼ teaspoon ground cardamom

Here's something you might not have thought of lately: an old-fashioned citrus custard that is superb on scones, English muffins, in tarts, with fruit or drizzled over cakes.

Wash jars and lids in hot soapy water; rinse well. Fill the jars with hot water.

In a bowl and using a fork, lightly beat the eggs until blended. Set aside.

Combine the sugar, orange and lemon juices, butter, orange zest and cardamom in the top pan of a double boiler or in a heatproof bowl. Set over (but not touching) simmering water and stir until the sugar dissolves and the butter melts.

Strain the beaten eggs through a fine-mesh sieve. Whisk into the juice-butter mixture. Cook, stirring constantly, until the custard thickens and leaves a path on the back of a spoon when a finger is drawn across, about 15 minutes; do not boil.

Drain 1 jar well. While the jar is still hot, spoon in the hot curd. Place a lid atop the jar; seal tightly. Repeat with the remaining curd and jars. Let cool to room temperature.

Store in the refrigerator for up to 3 weeks.

Makes about 1 pint (16 fl oz/500 ml)

Cappuccino Fudge Sauce

1 cup (8 fl oz/250 ml) half-and-half,
  or as needed

2 tablespoons freshly ground (medium-
  grind) coffee (not instant)

8 whole cloves

2 orange zest strips, each 2 inches
  (5 cm) long and 1 inch (2.5 cm) wide

1 cinnamon stick, about 3 inches
  (7.5 cm) long

⅛ teaspoon ground nutmeg

¼ cup (2 oz/60 g) plus 2 tablespoons
  firmly packed golden brown sugar

6 oz (185 g) bittersweet or semisweet
  chocolate, finely chopped

2 tablespoons brandy or Grand Marnier,
  optional

Redolent of coffee, chocolate and spice, this sauce makes a superb topping for vanilla, chocolate or coffee ice cream, slices of cake, or some combination of them. Spoon it into canning jars or ceramic containers, and include the following serving instructions on the gift card: Warm in a heavy saucepan over low heat, stirring constantly until just heated through.

Wash jars and lids in hot soapy water; rinse well. Fill the jars with hot water.

In a heavy saucepan over high heat, combine the 1 cup (8 fl oz/250 ml) half-and-half, the coffee, cloves, orange zest strips, cinnamon and nutmeg. Bring to a boil. Remove from the heat, cover and let stand for 30 minutes.

Return the mixture to high heat and again bring to a boil. Strain through a fine-mesh sieve into a measuring cup, pressing against the spices with the back of a wooden spoon to extract all the liquid. If necessary add more half-and-half to measure ¾ cup (6 fl oz/180 ml).

Pour the strained liquid into a clean, heavy saucepan. Add the brown sugar and simmer, stirring constantly, until dissolved. Remove from the heat. Add the chocolate and stir until melted and smooth. Stir in the brandy or Grand Marnier, if desired.

Drain 1 jar well. While the jar is still hot, spoon in the hot sauce. Place 1 lid atop the jar; seal tightly. Repeat with the remaining sauce and jars. Let cool to room temperature.

Store in the refrigerator for up to 2 weeks.

Makes about 1½ cups (12 fl oz/375 ml)

Pear and Cranberry Chutney

2 cups (14 oz/440 g) firmly packed
   golden brown sugar
¾ cup (3 oz/90 g) dried cranberries
½ cup (4 fl oz/125 ml) orange juice
½ cup (2½ oz/75 g) minced shallot
3 tablespoons minced, peeled fresh
   ginger
2 tablespoons balsamic vinegar
1 tablespoon finely grated orange zest
½ teaspoon ground cinnamon
⅜ teaspoon red pepper flakes
¼ teaspoon salt
1 lb (500 g) pears, peeled, cored and
   cut into ½-inch (12-mm) dice
4 cups (1 lb/500 g) fresh or frozen
   cranberries

*Here's something for the people on your list who like a little sweet
pizzazz with their savory treats: a spicy variation on cranberry
sauce that makes an excellent accompaniment to turkey, pork or
grilled chicken. For a slightly different flavor, substitute ¾ cup
(4½ oz/140 g) golden raisins for the dried cranberries.*

In a heavy nonaluminum saucepan over medium heat,
combine the brown sugar, dried cranberries, orange juice,
shallot, ginger, vinegar, orange zest, cinnamon, red pepper
flakes and salt. Stir until the sugar dissolves. Add the pears
and simmer, stirring occasionally, until the pears are tender,
about 10 minutes. Increase the heat to medium-high. Add
the fresh or frozen cranberries and boil, stirring frequently,
until they begin to burst, about 5 minutes.

   Meanwhile, wash canning jars and lids in hot soapy water;
rinse well. Fill the jars with hot water. Place the lids in a
small saucepan. Add water to cover and bring to a simmer.
Remove from the heat.

   Drain 1 jar. Spoon the hot chutney into the jar to within
¼ inch (6 mm) of the top. Run a nonmetallic spatula
between the chutney and the jar to remove air bubbles.
Using a towel dipped into hot water, immediately wipe the
rim clean. Drain 1 lid and place atop the jar; seal tightly
with the screw band. Repeat with the remaining chutney
and jars.

   Following the directions on page 11, process the jars in a
hot-water bath, check seals, label and store. (If the chutney
will be kept for no longer than 3 weeks, it is not necessary
to use a water bath. Simply store in the refrigerator.)

Makes about 2½ pints (40 fl oz/1.25 l)

Blueberry-Orange Marmalade

1½ cups (12 oz/375 g) granulated sugar
½ cup (4 fl oz/125 ml) fresh orange juice
2 cups (8 oz/250 g) fresh or frozen blueberries
3¼ cups (2 lb/1 kg) orange marmalade
1 teaspoon ground allspice

Purchased marmalade is the secret shortcut in this super-easy, super-tasty breakfast spread.

*I*n a heavy nonaluminum saucepan over low heat, combine the sugar and orange juice. Stir until the sugar dissolves. Raise the heat to medium-high and bring to a boil. Add the blueberries and boil, stirring frequently, until the mixture reaches the jelling stage, about 10 minutes. To test for doneness, remove from the heat. Fill a chilled spoon with the mixture, then slowly pour it back into the pan; the last 2 drops should merge and fall in a sheet. Alternatively, spoon 1 tablespoon of the mixture onto a chilled plate and place in the freezer for 2 minutes; it should wrinkle when gently pushed with a fingertip.

Add the marmalade and allspice to the blueberries. Clip a candy thermometer onto the pan and boil, stirring frequently, until it registers 220°F (104°C), about 15 minutes.

Meanwhile, wash canning jars and lids in hot soapy water; rinse well. Fill the jars with hot water. Place the lids in a small saucepan. Add water to cover and bring to a simmer. Remove from the heat.

Drain 1 jar. Spoon the hot marmalade into the jar to within ¼ inch (6 mm) of the top. Using a hot, damp towel, wipe the rim clean. Drain 1 lid and place atop the jar; seal tightly with the screw band. Repeat with the remaining marmalade and jars.

Following the directions on page 11, process the jars in a hot-water bath, check seals, label and store. (If the preserves will be kept for no longer than 3 weeks, it is not necessary to use a water bath. Simply store in the refrigerator.)

Makes about 2½ pints (40 fl oz/1.25 l)

Pine Nut and Honey Spread

1¼ cups (6½ oz/200 g) pine nuts
1¼ cups (15 oz/470 g) honey
2½ teaspoons finely grated orange zest
½ teaspoon ground cloves

Spread this soothing mixture on toasted country bread or English muffins for a breakfast or teatime treat. Use the best honey you can find, and, if desired, substitute ground cinnamon for the cloves.

Sterilize jars and lids according to the directions on page 10.

In a 4-cup (32-fl oz/1-l) glass measuring cup, combine the pine nuts, honey, orange zest and cloves and stir to mix well.

Using tongs, remove 1 jar from the water, draining well. Pour the honey spread into the jar. Remove 1 lid from the water and place atop the jar; seal tightly. Repeat with the remaining honey spread and jars.

Store at room temperature for up to 2 months. Mix well before using.

Makes about 2 cups (22 oz/685 g)

Pinenut -
Honey Spread

Chocolate, Caramel and Pecan Sauce

2½ cups (1¼ lb/625 g) granulated sugar

⅔ cup (5 fl oz/160 ml) water

1½ cups (12 fl oz/375 ml) heavy (double) cream

6 tablespoons (3 oz/90 g) unsalted butter

3 oz (90 g) semisweet chocolate, chopped

2 cups (8 oz/250 g) pecan halves and pieces

A luscious sauce combining creamy caramel and rich chocolate fudge is made even better when given a nutty pecan crunch. It can also be made with walnuts or toasted almonds and is superb over ice cream. For gift giving, enclose a card that reads: Before serving, warm in a heavy saucepan over low heat, stirring constantly and thinning with a small amount of water if necessary.

Wash jars and lids in hot soapy water; rinse well. Fill the jars with hot water.

In a deep, heavy saucepan over low heat, combine the sugar and the water. Stir until the sugar dissolves. Using a pastry brush dipped in water, brush down the sides of the pan to prevent sugar crystals from forming. Raise the heat to medium-high and bring to a boil. Continue to boil without stirring, swirling the pan occasionally, until the mixture turns a deep amber, about 15 minutes.

Remove from the heat. Add the cream (the mixture will bubble up; be careful to avoid splashes) and whisk until smooth. Return the pan to high heat and bring to a boil, whisking constantly. Remove from the heat, add the butter and chocolate and stir until melted and smooth. Stir in the pecans.

Drain 1 jar well. While the jar is still hot, spoon in the hot sauce. Place 1 lid atop the jar; seal tightly. Repeat with the remaining sauce and jars. Let cool to room temperature. Store in the refrigerator for up to 2 weeks.

Makes about 4 cups (32 fl oz/1 l)

Glossary

The following glossary defines terms specifically as they relate to making gifts of food, including major and unusual ingredients and basic techniques.

ALLSPICE
Sweet spice of Caribbean origin with a flavor suggesting a blend of **cinnamon, cloves** and **nutmeg,** hence its name. May be purchased as whole dried berries or ground. When using whole berries, they may be bruised—gently crushed with the bottom of a pan or other heavy instrument—to release more of their flavor.

ALMOND EXTRACT
Flavoring derived by dissolving the essential oil of almonds in an alcohol base. Use only products labeled "pure" or "natural" almond extract (essence).

BAY LEAVES
Dried whole leaves of the bay laurel tree. Pungent and spicy, they flavor pickling mixtures, marinades and simmered dishes. The French variety, sometimes available in specialty-food shops, has a milder, sweeter flavor, while California bay leaves are more assertive in character.

CARDAMOM
Sweet, exotic-tasting spice mainly used in Middle Eastern and Indian cooking and in Scandinavian baking. Its small, round seeds, which come enclosed inside a husklike pod, are best purchased whole, and the seeds ground as needed.

CAYENNE PEPPER
Very hot ground spice derived from dried cayenne chili peppers.

CHOCOLATE
When making candies, cookies, cakes or sauces, purchase the best-quality chocolate you can find—unsweetened, bittersweet, semisweet or sweet, as the recipe requires. Many cooks prefer the quality of European chocolate made in Switzerland, Belgium, France or Italy.

Unsweetened Chocolate
Pure cocoa liquor (half cocoa butter and half chocolate solids) ground and solidified in block-shaped molds. Unpalatable to some when eaten on its own, it provides intense chocolate flavor when combined with sugar and butter, milk or cream in recipes. Also known as bitter chocolate.

Bittersweet Chocolate
Lightly sweetened eating or baking chocolate that generally contains about 40 percent cocoa butter. Look for bittersweet chocolate that contains at least 50 percent cocoa butter.

Semisweet Chocolate
Eating or baking chocolate that is usually—but not always—slightly sweeter than bittersweet chocolate, which may be substituted.

Milk Chocolate
Primarily an eating chocolate, enriched with milk powder—the equivalent of up to 1 cup (8 fl oz/250 ml) whole milk in the average-sized candy bar.

White Chocolate
A chocolatelike product for eating or baking, made by combining pure cocoa butter with sugar, powdered milk and sometimes vanilla. Check labels to make sure that the white chocolate you buy is made exclusively with cocoa butter, without the addition of coconut oil or vegetable shortening.

Chocolate Chips
Any of several kinds of chocolate—usually semisweet, bittersweet, milk or white—molded into small drop shapes, for uniform incorporation into doughs or batters.

Unsweetened Cocoa
Richly flavored, fine-textured powder ground from the solids left after much of the cocoa butter has been extracted from chocolate liquor. Cocoa powder specially treated to reduce its natural acidity, resulting in a darker color and more mellow flavor, is known as Dutch-process cocoa.

To Chop Chocolate
While a food processor fitted with the metal blade can be used, a sharp, heavy knife offers better control. First, break the chocolate by hand into small chunks, handling it as little as possible to avoid melting. Then, using a heavy knife and a clean, dry, odor-free chopping surface, carefully chop into smaller pieces.

Steadying the knife with your hand, continue chopping across the pieces until the desired consistency is reached.

To Melt Chocolate
Put pieces of chocolate in the top pan of a double boiler over barely simmering water, taking care that the pan doesn't touch the water or that the water does not create steam. Stir gently until the chocolate has melted.

Alternatively, create your own double boiler by placing a heatproof bowl on top of a pan of simmering water.

CHILI PEPPERS, DRIED RED
In their dried form, several different varieties of small, ripened red chilies—sold in Latin American markets and well-stocked food stores—are used as seasonings to impart moderate to hot spiciness to foods. When handling any chili, wear kitchen gloves to prevent any cuts or abrasions on your hands from contacting the pepper's volatile oils; wash your hands well with warm, soapy water after handling, and take special care not to touch your eyes or any other sensitive areas.

CINNAMON
Popular sweet spice for flavoring. The aromatic bark of a type of evergreen tree, it is sold as whole dried strips—cinnamon sticks—or ground.

CLOVES
Rich and aromatic East African spice used whole or in its ground form to flavor both sweet and savory recipes.

COCONUT
For baking purposes, shredded or flaked coconut is sold ready to use in cans or plastic packages in the baking section of most food stores. The label indicates whether the product is sweetened or unsweetened; most dessert recipes call for sweetened coconut. Be sure to purchase coconut products from a store with a rapid turnover, to ensure freshness. Some recipes call for toasting flaked coconut to develop its flavor: Spread the flakes evenly on a baking sheet and bake in a 350°F (180°C) oven, stirring occasionally, until pale gold, 10–20 minutes.

COFFEE, GROUND
When a recipe calls for ground coffee, you'll get the fullest, finest flavor by freshly grinding coffee beans yourself as you need them. An adjustable burr-type grinder, which actually crushes the beans to a preset particle size, is fairly expensive. If using a common and relatively inexpensive electric blade-type grinder, a medium grind is usually achieved in about 10 seconds of continual grinding; finely ground coffee results from 15–20 seconds of grinding.

CORIANDER
Small, spicy-sweet seeds of the coriander plant, which is also called cilantro or Chinese parsley. Used whole or ground as a seasoning, particularly in Middle Eastern and Indian cuisines.

CORN SYRUP
Light- or dark-colored, neutral-tasting syrup extracted from corn.

CRANBERRIES
Round, deep red, tart berries, grown primarily in wet, sandy coastal lands—or bogs—in the northeastern United States. Available fresh during the late autumn, and frozen year-round.

Dried cranberries, resembling raisins in shape, are available in specialty-food stores.

CREAM, HEAVY
Whipping cream with a butterfat content of at least 36 percent. For the best flavor and cooking properties, purchase 100 percent natural fresh cream with a short shelf life; avoid long-lasting varieties that have been processed by ultraheat methods. In Britain, use double cream.

CUMIN
Middle Eastern spice with a strong, dusky, aromatic flavor, popular in cuisines of its region of origin along with those of Latin America, India and parts of Europe. Sold either ground or as whole, small, crescent-shaped seeds.

CURRANTS, DRIED
Produced from a small variety of grapes, these dried fruits resemble tiny raisins but have a tarter flavor. Sold in the baking section of food stores.

FENNEL SEEDS
Small, crescent-shaped seeds of a plant related to the bulb vegetable of the same name, prized as a spice for their mild anise flavor.

FIGS, DRIED
Moist dried fruits with a rich flavor and chewy texture. The golden Calimyrna variety has a sweet, nutty flavor that is particularly prized in baked goods and preserves.

FLOUR, ALL-PURPOSE
The most common flour for baking purposes is all-purpose flour (also called plain flour), a blend of hard and soft wheats available in all food markets. All-purpose flour is sold in its natural, pale yellow unbleached form or bleached, the result of a chemical process that not only whitens it but also makes it easier to blend with higher percentages of fat and sugar. Bleached flour is therefore commonly used for recipes where more tender results are desired, while unbleached flour yields more crisp results.

GINGER
The rhizome of the tropical ginger plant, which yields a sweet, strong-flavored spice. Whole ginger rhizomes (below), commonly but mistakenly called roots, may be purchased fresh in a food store or vegetable market. Ginger pieces are available crystallized or candied in specialty-food shops or the baking or Asian sections of well-stocked food stores. Ginger preserved in syrup is sold in specialty shops or in Asian food sections. Ground, dried ginger is easily found in jars or tins in the food store spice section.

GRAND MARNIER
A popular commercial brand of orange-flavored liqueur, distinguished by its pure Cognac base.

HALF-AND-HALF
A commercial dairy product consisting of half milk and half light cream. Known as half cream in Britain.

MAPLE SYRUP, PURE
Syrup made from boiling the sap of the maple tree, with an inimitably rich savor and intense sweetness. Buy maple syrup that is labeled "pure," rather than a blend.

MARSHMALLOW CREME
Bottled commercial product, available in most food stores, made from the same ingredients as the fluffy candies with which it shares a name: beaten egg whites, gelatin and sugar syrup. Used as a dessert topping for ice creams, an easy cake frosting or an ingredient in other sweet recipes.

Nuts

Rich and mellow in flavor, crisp and crunchy in texture, a wide variety of nuts are used in foods made for gift giving. For the best selection, look in a specialty-food shop, health-food store or the food store baking section. Some of the most popular options include:

Almonds

Mellow, sweet-flavored nuts (below) that are an important crop in California and are popular throughout the world.

Cashews

Kidney-shaped, crisp nuts with a slightly sweet and buttery flavor. Native to tropical America but grown throughout the world, primarily India.

Hazelnuts

Small, usually spherical nuts (below) with a slightly sweet flavor. Grown in Italy, Spain and the United States. Also known as filberts.

Macadamias

Spherical nuts, about twice the diameter of hazelnuts, with a very rich, buttery flavor and crisp texture. Native to Australia, they are now grown primarily in Hawaii.

Peanuts

Not true nuts, these are actually legumes that grow on a low-branching plant. When roasted, they have a rich, full flavor and satisfying crispness that make them the world's most popular nut.

Pecans

Brown-skinned, crinkly textured nuts (below) with a distinctive sweet, rich flavor and crisp, slightly crumbly texture. Native to the southern United States.

Pine Nuts

Small ivory seeds extracted from the cones of a species of pine tree, with a rich, slightly resinous flavor.

Walnuts

Rich, crisp-textured nuts (below) with distinctively crinkled surfaces. English walnuts, the most familiar variety, are grown worldwide, although the largest crops are in California. American black walnuts, sold primarily as shelled pieces, have a stronger flavor that lends extra distinction to desserts and candies.

To Blanch Nuts

Some nuts, such as almonds, require blanching to loosen their papery skins. To blanch nuts, put them in a pan of boiling water for about 2 minutes; then drain and, when they are cool enough to handle, squeeze each nut between your fingers to slip it from its skin.

To Toast Nuts

Toasting brings out the full flavor and aroma of nuts. To toast any kind of nut, preheat an oven to 325°F (165°C). Spread the nuts in a single layer on a baking sheet and toast in the oven until they just begin to change color, 5–10 minutes. Remove from the oven and let cool to room temperature.

Toasting also loosens the skins of nuts such as hazel-nuts and walnuts, which may be removed by wrapping the still-warm nuts in a cotton towel and rubbing against them with the palms of your hands.

To Chop Nuts

To chop nuts, spread them in a single layer on a nonslip cutting surface. Using a chef's knife, carefully chop the nuts with a gentle rocking motion.

Alternatively, put a handful or two of nuts in a food processor fitted with the metal blade and use a few rapid on-off pulses to chop the nuts to desired consistency; repeat with the remaining nuts in batches. Be careful not to process the nuts too long or their oils will be released and the nuts will turn into a paste.

Milk, Condensed

Whole milk from which approximately 60 percent of the water has been removed, resulting in an intensified flavor and consistency that enriches some dessert recipes. Sweetened condensed milk includes sugar.

Molasses

Thick, robust-tasting, syrupy sugarcane by-product of sugar refining. Light molasses results from the first boiling of the syrup; dark molasses from the second boiling.

Nutmeg

Popular baking spice that is the hard pit of the fruit of the nutmeg tree. May be bought already ground or, for fresher flavor, whole.

Oil, Olive

Extra-virgin olive oil, extracted from olives on the first pressing without use of heat or chemicals, is valued for its distinctive fruity flavor. Many brands, varying in color and strength of flavor, are now available; choose one that suits your taste. The higher-priced extra-virgin olive oils usually are of better quality. Store in an airtight container away from heat and light.

Oil, Vegetable

The term "vegetable oil" refers to any of several refined pure or blended oils pressed or otherwise extracted from any of a number of sources—including corn, cottonseed, peanuts, safflower seeds, soybeans and sunflower seeds—and prized for their pale color, neutral flavor and the high temperature to which they can be heated.

Olives

Throughout Mediterranean Europe, olives are cured in

combinations of salt, seasonings, brines, vinegars and oils to produce pungently flavored results. Good-quality cured black olives, such as Greek Kalamata, French Niçoise and Italian Gaeta varieties, and green olives, such as French and Spanish varieties, are available in ethnic delicatessens, specialty-food shops and well-stocked food stores.

ORANGE PEEL, CANDIED
Strips of orange peel, usually including some of the white pith, that have been saturated with sugar syrup and then dried. Available in the baking section of well-stocked markets and in specialty-food stores.

PECORINO CHEESE
Italian sheep's milk cheese, sold either fresh or aged. Two of its most popular aged forms are pecorino romano and pecorino sardo; the latter cheese is tangier than the former.

PEPPER
Pepper, the most common of all savory spices, is best purchased as whole peppercorns, to be ground in a pepper mill as needed, or coarsely crushed or cracked using a mortar and pestle or the flat side of a heavy knife.

RED PEPPER FLAKES
Coarsely ground flakes of dried red chilies, including seeds, that add moderately hot flavor to the foods they season.

ROSEMARY
Mediterranean herb, used fresh or dried, with a strong aromatic flavor. Sprigs of fresh rosemary make an attractive flavoring in bottled oils and vinegars and in marinades.

SHALLOTS
Small member of the onion family with brown skin, white-to-purple flesh and a flavor resembling a cross between sweet onion and garlic.

STAR ANISE
A small, hard, brown seedpod resembling an eight-pointed star (below), used whole or broken into individual points to lend its distinctive anise flavor to savory or sweet dishes. The spokes of the star contain small seeds.

VANILLA
One of the most popular flavorings in dessert making. Vanilla beans are dried aromatic pods of a variety of orchid. But vanilla is most commonly used in the form of an alcohol-based extract (essence); be sure to purchase products labeled "pure vanilla extract." Vanilla extract or beans from Madagascar are of the best quality.

VINEGARS
Literally "sour wine," vinegar results when certain strains of yeast cause wine—or some other alcoholic liquid such as apple cider or Japanese rice wine—to ferment for a second time, turning it acidic. The best-quality wine vinegars begin with good-quality wine. Red wine vinegar, like the wine from which it is made, has a more robust flavor than vinegar produced from white wine; Champagne vinegar, prized for its delicacy, is produced not from the sparkling wine of that name but from still white wine of the same region. Balsamic vinegar, a specialty of Modena, Italy, is a vinegar made from reduced grape juice and is aged for many years.

YEAST
Active dry yeast is one of the most widely available forms of yeast for baking, commonly sold in individual packages containing a scant 1 tablespoon (¼ oz/7 g) and found in the baking section of food stores. Seek out one of the new strains of quick-rise yeast available in specialty-food stores.

ZEST
Thin, brightly colored, outermost layer of a citrus fruit's peel, containing most of its aromatic essential oils—a lively source of flavor. Zest may be removed using one of two easy methods:

1. Use a simple tool known as a zester, drawing its sharp-edged holes across the fruit's skin to remove the zest in thin strips. Alternatively, use a fine hand-held grater.

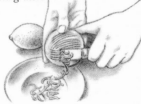

2. Holding the edge of a paring knife or vegetable peeler away from you and almost parallel to the fruit's skin, carefully cut off the zest in thin strips, taking care not to remove any white pith with it. Then use as is, or thinly slice or chop on a cutting board.

SUGARS
Many different forms of sugar are used to sweeten and decorate baked goods and candies.

Brown Sugar
A rich-tasting, fine-textured granulated sugar combined with molasses in varying quantities to yield golden, light or dark brown sugar.

Granulated Sugar
The standard, widely used form of pure white sugar. Do not use superfine granulated sugar unless specified. In Britain, caster sugar is a good substitute for American granulated sugar.

Colored Sugar Crystals
Relatively large crystals of sugar colored with natural vegetable dyes and sprinkled onto finished baked goods for decoration.

Confectioners' Sugar
Finely pulverized sugar, also known as powdered or icing sugar, which dissolves quickly and provides a thin, white decorative coating. To prevent confectioners' sugar from absorbing moisture in the air and caking, manufacturers often mix a little cornstarch into it.

Pearl Sugar
Large crystals of sugar polished to a pearllike sheen and smoothness for use as a decoration.

Index

almonds
  chocolate-almond caramels 23
  cranberry-almond biscotti 39
  milk chocolate and toasted-
    almond fudge 16
amaretti, hazelnut 56

bell peppers in flavored oil,
  roasted 68
biscotti
  chocolate-walnut biscotti 53
  cranberry-almond biscotti 39
blueberry-orange marmalade 98
bread
  fig and walnut pumpkin bread 61
  raisin, cherry and apricot
    panettone 62
breadsticks, fennel, Parmesan and
  pepper 49
brittle, pine nut 25
brownies, triple-chocolate 46

cakes
  currant, lemon and ginger cake 50
  miniature chocolate chip and
    coconut cakes 54
cappuccino fudge sauce 94
caramel-nut popcorn 20
caramels
  chocolate-almond caramels 23
  vanilla bean caramels 15
chocolate
  cappuccino fudge sauce 94
  chocolate, caramel and pecan
    sauce 102
  chocolate, nut and fig panforte 43
  chocolate-almond caramels 23
  chocolate coating 8
  chocolate-walnut biscotti 53

double-chocolate and orange
  truffles 27
espresso, white chocolate and
  macadamia nut bark 28
fancy chocolate chunk-oatmeal
  cookies 58
macadamia and coconut
  clusters 36
milk chocolate and toasted-
  almond fudge 16
miniature chocolate chip and
  coconut cakes 54
pecan-molasses toffee 32
scones with chocolate chips and
  dried cherries 64
triple-chocolate brownies 46
walnut-date clusters 19
walnut-raisin fudge 30
chutneys
  dried-fruit chutney 89
  pear and cranberry chutney 97
cider sachets, hot spiced 72
coconut
  macadamia and coconut
    clusters 36
  miniature chocolate chip and
    coconut cakes 54
cookies
  chocolate-walnut biscotti 53
  cranberry-almond biscotti 39
  fancy chocolate chunk-oatmeal
    cookies 58
  hazelnut amaretti 56
  holiday orange-spice cutouts 40
  vanilla and walnut shortbread
    hearts 44
cranberries
  cranberry-almond biscotti 39
  pear and cranberry chutney 97
curd, orange-lemon 93
currant, lemon and ginger cake 50

date-walnut clusters 19

equipment 6–7
espresso, white chocolate and
  macadamia nut bark 28

fennel, Parmesan and pepper
  breadsticks 49
figs
  chocolate, nut and fig panforte
    43
  fig and walnut pumpkin bread 61
fudge
  milk chocolate and toasted-
    almond fudge 16
  walnut-raisin fudge 30

hazelnut amaretti 56
honey spread, pine nut and 100

icing, confectioners' sugar 9

jams and preserves
  blueberry-orange marmalade 98
  peaches and spice jam 90
  plum-vanilla preserves 85

kitchen potpourri 79

lemon glaze 8

macadamia nuts
  espresso, white chocolate and
    macadamia nut bark 28
  macadamia and coconut
    clusters 36
maple-nut pralines 35
marmalade, blueberry-orange 98

nuts, spiced 81

olive oil with lemon and bay leaf
  76
olives
  lemon-spice olives 82
  olives with orange and fennel 75

panettone, raisin, cherry and
  apricot 62

panforte, chocolate, nut and fig 43
peaches-and-spice jam 90
peach vinegar 71
pear and cranberry chutney 97
pecans
  chocolate, caramel and pecan
    sauce 102
  pecan-molasses toffee 32
pine nut and honey spread 100
plum-vanilla preserves 85
popcorn, caramel-nut 20
potpourri, kitchen 79
pralines, maple-nut 35
pumpkin bread, fig and walnut 61

raisins
  raisin, cherry and apricot
    panettone 62
  walnut-raisin fudge 30
raspberry-red wine sauce 86

sauces
  cappuccino fudge sauce 94
  chocolate, caramel and pecan
    sauce 102
  raspberry-red wine sauce 86
scones with chocolate chips and
  dried cherries 64

toffee, pecan-molasses 32
truffles, double-chocolate and
  orange 27

vinegars
  orange and rosemary vinegar 67
  peach vinegar 71

walnuts
  chocolate-walnut biscotti 53
  fig and walnut pumpkin bread 61
  vanilla and walnut shortbread
    hearts 44
  walnut-date clusters 19
  walnut-raisin fudge 30

ACKNOWLEDGMENTS

The publishers would like to thank the following people and organizations for their generous assistance and support in producing this book:
William Garry, James Badham, Gretchen McFarlan, Sonja Inglin, Sharon C. Lott, Stephen W. Griswold, Ken DellaPenta, Tarji Mickelson, Jennifer Hauser, Jennifer Mullins, the buyers for Gardener's Eden, and the buyers and store managers for Hold Everything, Pottery Barn and Williams-Sonoma stores.

The following kindly lent props for the photography:
Biordi Art Imports, California Walnuts, Candelier, Fillamento, Fredericksen Hardware, J. Goldsmith Antiques,
Green Valley Growers, Sue Fisher King, Lorraine Puckett, RH, and Chuck Williams.